*A Handicapped Child
in the Family*

A GUIDE FOR PARENTS

To my parents
whose wisdom, courage, and reliability
provided a sound foundation

and to my husband, Bill
whose depth of love and understanding has
contributed so much to my actualization as a person

Contents

Foreword

When it dawns upon parents that their child is to grow up handi-capped—sometimes evident at birth or shortly thereafter, but per-haps only after several years of normal development—the parents face a nearly overwhelming psychological problem. This book is for these parents; it helps them to see that the problems are not theirs alone but have been faced by many other parents across the country. Here—through sensitive accounts of the shattered dreams of parents, of their desires to make every sacrifice required for the happiness of their children, of their guilt over their occasional re-sentment that the helpless child has so deeply affected the conduct of their lives—parents can find a larger context in which to meet the common demands of providing for the handicapped child's happi-ness and optimal development, while permitting the parents to live their own lives in ways that will lead to the contentment that all human beings deserve. Then, too, there are the brothers and sisters of the handicapped child. They, like their parents, are in conflict over how to be thoughtful of and attentive to the handicapped sibling while at the same time living their own lives and fulfilling their own aspirations.

A physical handicap has to be understood and dealt with as such, but it inevitably has psychological and social consequences, both direct and indirect. The direct consequences are reflected in the limitations upon behavior, often requiring dependence upon others, and some activities that cannot be engaged in. But there are also indirect consequences that come about because of the handicap and the ways in which other people react to it. All children have a struggle with independence from adults, but this struggle is accentuated for the child whose relation to parents is unusually intimate and dependent over the years of development. Other people react to visible handicaps in social ways that go beyond the limitation that the handicap imposes. The author, herself severely handicapped by polio as a child, gives a meaningful account of her own struggle against a well-meaning vocational rehabilitation director and a university Dean of Women, both of whom tried to prevent her from going to college because of her physical limitations. She overcame their objections and eventually proved that her handicaps did not prevent her achieving a Ph.D., and that she was able to go ahead to a successful professional career.

I was head of Stanford's psychology department and one of her professors while she was in graduate study; that is how I happen to be writing this foreword. I saw then how well she and her husband had teamed up to work out professional lives for both of them despite the severity of her physical limitations, and it has been heartening to see how well their hopes have been fulfilled in the years since.

The approach of this book through the reports of parents participating in group therapy—the reports commonly in their own words—turns out to be a very instructive one. It shows how their own attitudes, at first defensive and distorting their inner feelings, gradually became modified through the sharing of common experiences. Thus, what may have begun as a feeling of hopelessness and helplessness gradually turns into realistic problem-solving. It is not necessary to be Pollyanna-like ("everything is for the best") in order to see some spots of sunshine among the shadows, and to act accordingly.

The book is written with a minimum of technical jargon. It communicates through concrete life situations of real people, and their expressed feelings, rather than through technical labels or cookbook "how-to-do-it" instructions. The people come alive in these accounts, and their messages are clear.

Parents of a handicapped child can only have their vision broadened and their options increased through reading this book. They will identify and empathize with the many other parents who are as baffled as they; they will feel a sense of community with them, and will end up seeming less alone as they face the needs of their handicapped child, and their own needs, as they seek to find some path towards maximum happiness for all those who are involved.

Ernest R. Hilgard, Ph.D.
Professor Emeritus of Psychology,
Stanford University

Palo Alto, California

Preface

The work upon which this book is based first came to life as a creative idea in the mind of Mr. John Simmons, while he was President of United Cerebral Palsy Foundation of San Diego County. It stemmed from his deep and personal concern for the psychological development of the handicapped child and from his conviction of the importance of parental influence.

When Mr. Simmons asked me to plan and conduct a group devoted to the counseling and/or education of parents with regard to their handicapped children, I explained that I would like to work with these parents as their psychotherapist, trying to help them in the same ways that I help my private patients. My approach came from my own conviction that parent-child relationships are so much determined at deeper motivational levels that any direction I might give parents about how to relate to their children would be ineffective unless I could attempt to integrate this with work on the parents' own problems.

I conducted the resulting therapy group for parents of cerebral palsied children for approximately one year under the auspices of the local agency and for a second year under a research grant from the national organization, United Cerebral Palsy Research and Educational Foundation, Inc. A second research grant was awarded to cover evaluation of the tape recordings of the therapy sessions. My appreciation therefore goes particularly to Mr. Simmons and to Brewster S. Miller, M.D. (then Director of Research and Medical Director of the national foundation). Both gave continuing support throughout the project. I owe a special debt of gratitude to the parents who, as members of the therapy group, kindly gave their consent to the utilization of this material for publication.

Over the years so many people have contributed to my personal and professional development that it is impossible to thank all of them here. Among these, I wish to acknowledge with special gratitude my indebtedness to Dr. Ernest R. Hilgard, from whom I received inspiration and help at several crucial points in my training and career.

Three secretaries have worked on my original research report and the manuscript of this book, and each has been steadfastly reliable and efficient. I wish to thank Sharon R. Shepherd, Rita Marie Homewood, and Kathryn Griffiths Smith.

Verda Heisler

San Diego, California

Introduction

This is a book for parents of handicapped children. It is the product of a therapy group I conducted over a two-year period with parents of cerebral palsied children. But, in a broader sense, it is the product of more than that, for it draws upon two longer and more comprehensive realms of experience in my own life. One of these is the professional realm of twenty years of full-time practice in helping people, through psychotherapy, with a myriad of personal and family adjustment problems. The other is my own personal experience as a physically handicapped person. At the age of eight, I had a severe case of poliomyelitis, and my experiential knowledge of the meaning of adjustment to physical handicap is therefore drawn from both childhood and adult years.

This book is intended to be of help not only to parents of cerebral palsied children, but to those whose children suffer any kind of physical or mental handicap. These children may have such diverse problems as polio, muscular dystrophy, mental deficiency, respiratory and cardiac ailments, speech and hearing defects, or organic brain damage. Many of the principles set forth apply also to the general adjustment problems of childhood, but the book does not center on these. That one book, written for parents, can be relevant to such diverse childhood conditions results from the fact that the focus of the book is on the *psychological* adjustment of the parents to the special problem of their child's handicap.

Those who work with handicapped children and their families know that most childhood handicaps present a many-faceted problem, requiring a multidisciplinary approach. A particular discipline, such as physical therapy, will be relevant to some of the conditions mentioned above but not to others. Even among those for which physical therapy is relevant, the application of this discipline varies. A physical therapist writing for parents of cerebral palsied children would present material different from that presented by a physical therapist writing for parents of children with polio or muscular dystrophy. A medical doctor explaining the care and treatment of a cardiac impairment would say different things than would a doctor explaining the care and treatment of asthma. But in the matter of the *psychological* adjustment of the parents to the problem, the same principles are applicable to all.

The basic principles of psychological health and adjustment do not vary according to the specific problem that life brings to the individual. The same principles of human functioning that are mobilized by any of life's challenges are mobilized by the problem of handicap, and this is true with regard both to the child's adjustment to his own handicap and to the parents' adjustment to the child's handicap. The child's handicap imposes upon him certain limitations of functioning and of life experience, and these limitations vary according to the nature and severity of the impairment. Thus, in addition to meeting the everyday challenges to psychological adjustment met by nonhandicapped persons, the physically handicapped individual must reconcile himself to his special deprivation and frustration, and must maximize his potential for living within the framework of limitations imposed by his disability. His success in this struggle will be determined by those factors which influence the development of his personality and his level of psychological self-actualization.

Any parent who turns with interest to this book will do so out of concern for the happiness and optimal functioning of his or her child. The parent who reads this book will do so from a realization that, as a parent, he or she wields an extremely significant influence on the life and development of the child. Psychologists have contributed to a widespread recognition that the family is the primary agent of the formation of the patterns of personality. In ways of which they are most often unconscious, parents are involved in the creation of their child's formative experiences, and the significant psychological interchanges are more often covert than overt. What kind of person the parent is will constitute a more powerful influence than what he does.

People often hold to the fallacious belief that the child is deeply affected only by that which he consciously realizes and is able to remember. This belief results from a lack of understanding of the great extent to which psychological processes take place unconsciously. This belief is often accompanied by the equally fallacious view that the parent can prevent the child from being affected by certain of the parent's attitudes and feelings by not letting the child know about them. This viewpoint does not recognize the fact that the most powerful communication between parent and child takes place unconsciously and nonverbally. Children, like little animals, have a natural intuitive capacity which reaches through and past the boundaries of the spoken word and the conscious act.

The power of unconscious determinants is an unacceptable premise to those who want to believe that all aspects of their functioning are under their conscious control. Life is full of paradoxes, and the truly striking paradox here is that only by recognizing the power of the unconscious, taking it into account, and working with it can one extend one's sphere of conscious awareness and control.

The parent of the handicapped child may realize that the child's adjustment to his handicap will be either facilitated or limited by the parent's reactions to and ways of coping with the problem. Realizing this—and feeling strongly motivated to facilitate his handicapped child's adjustment and development—the parent may want to be told how he *should* react and how he *should* cope with the problems handicap brings. Quite reasonably, he wants to be given guidelines for behavior.

It is not the purpose of this book (nor, indeed, is it possible) to attempt to present such guidelines or general principles. It is, instead, a basic premise of this book that the ways in which the parents react to and cope with their child's handicap will be determined by their own psychological dynamics, life orientation, and level of actualization as individuals. The problem of the child's handicap will call forth his parent's characteristic and individual ways of functioning just as will any life problem. From this basic premise, a second is derived: that the best way to help the parent facing this special life problem is to help him in his overall functioning as an individual. The better he is able to understand his own feelings and to act upon this understanding, the better able he will be to relate to the problem of his child's handicap in a healthy and constructive way. The child will absorb the benefits of his parents' self-development.

These were the premises upon which I have based my work with the parents of cerebral palsied children. Before starting that therapy group, I searched the literature on past group work with parents of handicapped children and found substantiation for my viewpoint. Over the last two decades, various group approaches to the problem have been tried and reported. While none of these groups was set up with the purpose of providing psychotherapy to help these parents with their own adjustment as individuals, all of them encountered individual adjustment problems on the part of the parents as inescapable factors in the situation.

For example, parental patterns which are common sources of family problems among the general population have been found to be intensified in the parental relationship with the handicapped child. These parental patterns include parental narcissism, rejection, and overprotection; identification of the children with the parents' siblings; parental identification of the children with themselves; feelings of inadequacy, masochism, compulsiveness, and obsessive anxiety.[1] Greenberg recommended the sharing of problems by parents of handicapped children through groups.

One recent study compared the concerns of handicapped young adults with those of mothers of handicapped young adults.[2] The subjects were seen in separate small discussion groups. Some of the parents and offspring were from the same family and others were not. According to the author, "The most serious concerns of both groups were in two areas usually worked through and more or less solved by late adolescence—the achievement of independence from the family and the handling of sexuality." Separation anxiety was much more pronounced in the mothers than in the offspring, in many instances stemming from unresolved guilt feelings over unconscious resentment of the burden. This parental conflict was often manifested through excessive limitation of the young adults' independence, and also found expression in the mothers' negative attitudes toward their offspring's sexual interests. The study states:

> Apparently the typical mother had not completed the work of "mourning" the lost dream of having a normal child. The natural grief, anger, shame, and guilt which inevitably arise with such a disappointment had left a powerful residue. Far from being faced, expressed, and assimilated, the mourning had never been completed, and the feelings had been fought and defended against over the years. Denial of the negative feelings and reaction-formation against them were the chief defenses, leading to the inhibition of affect and the unrealistic efforts to help and to keep the children close. Guilt, over-protection, and resentment seemed to feed upon each other in a never-ending underground cycle.

Studies such as these reaffirm the viewpoint that parents will not be helped a great deal by simply providing them with guidelines for action. Genuine help for these parents must be of a kind that provides them with the opportunity for exploring and bringing to light all of the unhappy feelings they have not been able to face and resolve without such help. Since the ways in which a particular parent experiences this trauma are interrelated with other problems and patterns in his personality, the therapist must be ready to work with the parent on any problem that comes up. In my search of the literature, I did not find any report of group therapy set up in this way for parents of handicapped children. In some instances, a more limited counseling was done.[3] In another, the author recommended the method of parent education, which she differentiated from group therapy in this way: "Although parents are encouraged to recognize their feelings as well as the facts, group education explores only those feelings which are conscious (or nearly so) and experienced by many; it does not deal with unconscious factors nor attempt to work through pathological areas of the parents' own problems."[4]

The closest approach to genuine group therapy with this special parent population was reported in a comprehensive account of dynamically oriented small discussion groups involving a total of fifty families and extending in time from five months to two years. The researcher summarizes his conclusions as follows:

> This method of attempting to evaluate and resolve emotional difficulties in the family of the handicapped child can only be regarded at this time as an experiment. . . . Although reality factors are obviously present and important in attempting to understand parental feelings toward the cerebral palsied child, this study reveals that reality factors alone are quite insufficient to account for the gamut of perceptions and feelings which parents show; and it would, therefore, be erroneous to base planning for the needs of the handicapped child and his family upon reality factors alone. . . . The parents of children with cerebral palsy . . . do not, as a rule, seek psychological help for themselves. . . . They nevertheless are in need of help because their attitudes and behavior, often unconsciously determined, influence in a very specific and definite way the psychological development of their children. How such parents can gain sufficient motivation to look at the way in which their attitudes and behavior reflect upon the child and family has been of major concern. The parent of the child with cerebral palsy has a vast array of external circumstances upon which to project and rationalize almost all of his feelings and behavior, and it is probably for this reason that individual help is so infrequently sought.[5]

My own view is that the best way to facilitate family adjustment to the special handicap of a child is through psychotherapy with the parents. While I would recommend either individual or group therapy for this purpose, the therapy group does have the advantage of enabling the parents to help each other with problems specific to handicap and not shared by the general population. This kind of sharing breaks through the sense of isolation that envelops those experiencing a special problem.

My therapy group for parents of cerebral palsied children was conducted under a research grant from United Cerebral Palsy Research and Educational Foundation, Inc. The question under consideration was whether a group of parents brought together on the basis of the common problem of having children with cerebral palsy would utilize the available therapy for their own growth, and whether evidence could be found of indirect benefit to the handicapped child through such personal growth of the parent. As in all therapy groups, the participants varied in the ways and the extent to which they entered into the therapeutic process. These variations were a function of the personality structures and psychological defense systems of the group members. In the case of those members who did utilize the therapeutic opportunity, their children seemed to benefit.

This book is not a full report of the research study, nor is it a comprehensive treatment of the subject of parental adjustment to a child's handicap. It is, instead, a book written for parents with the purpose of awakening their awareness of the fuller and deeper meanings of their reactions to their child's handicap and the problems it brings. It attempts to stimulate parental awareness through the use of illustrative material drawn from my research group. Through the pages of this book, a mother will enter the therapeutic experiences of other mothers struggling with similar problems, and she will find herself through what she reads. These glimpses into the inner worlds of other parents will bring the reader a new perspective on his or her own adjustment problems. Parents will begin to look inward rather than outward for the meaning of their emotional distress, tension, irritability, or depression, and this initiation of a process of self-exploration will, in turn, enable them to view their handicapped child in a new light. If they are able to maintain the inner focus, they will begin to discover inner resources for coping with what had previously seemed like insurmountable external realities.

It is my hope that this book will move many parents toward a quest for deeper understanding of the problem of handicap in which life has involved them. General statements can be made about the meaning of such a problem, but genuine understanding of it cannot be achieved at a purely intellectual level. The kind of understanding which will most constructively influence the course of a child's life is achieved by the parent in a way that integrates emotions, experience, and understanding. The parents who are stimulated by this book to pursue this quest with real involvement will want therapeutic help, and it is therefore also the purpose of the book to promote the formation of therapy groups by those agencies across the country which are currently serving the handicapped child and his family.

BIBLIOGRAPHY

1. H. A. Greenberg: Problems of parents of handicapped children. *Journal of Exceptional Children*, 17, 1:1–7, October 1950.
2. M. H. Mowatt: Emotional conflicts of handicapped young adults and their mothers. *Cerebral Palsy Journal*, 26, 4:6–8, July-August 1965. Quoted by permission.
3. H. O. Bice and M. G. D. Holden: Group counseling with mothers of children with cerebral palsy. *Journal of Social Casework*, March 1949.
4. A. B. Auerbach: What can parents of handicapped children gain from group experience? In: *Helping Parents of Handicapped Children: Group Approaches*. Boston, Child Study Association of America, 1959, p. 18.
5. J. D. Call: Psychological problems of the cerebral palsied child, his parents and siblings as revealed by dynamically oriented small group discussions with parents. *Cerebral Palsy Review*, September-October 1958, p. 15. Quoted by permission.

CHAPTER ONE

Help with Emotional Adjustment

"I have something I would like to say. Mark came home the other day from his physical therapy feeling so good about the progress he is making, and I couldn't help remembering how he used to hate to go and how he used to fight against exercising at all. Then I thought about the change in my own feelings." The young woman speaking was tall, slim, clear-eyed, and attractive. She was addressing her remarks to a group of about ten parents, seated in a circle and listening intently.

"I'm most aware of the change in myself when I help Mark with his bath," she continued. "I noticed yesterday that this didn't seem such a difficult task any more. But the change was really in me! I didn't feel angry or mean or resentful. I just felt plain good. I don't hate it any more. It's a good feeling inside to feel—I don't know how to say it or how to express it—but to really feel deep down inside that I'm simply glad that I'm here, and I'm glad to be alive, and I'm glad I've got Mark. I may have said these things before, but I don't think I ever meant them truly. I do now. And I'm glad."

As the session came to an end and the parents departed, my own thoughts went back about ten months to my initial meeting with Lois. At the request of the local affiliate of United Cerebral

Palsy, I was interviewing parents interested in joining with other parents of handicapped children for weekly group sessions in which they would have an opportunity to work on problems of family adjustment. Lois and her husband, Gilbert, impressed me as a particularly bright and earnest young couple, strongly motivated to meet the special needs of their seven-year-old, cerebral palsied son in the best possible way. Mark's handicap involved moderate spasticity, which affected the functioning of both his hands and legs and necessitated the use of braces and crutches.

As all parents of physically handicapped children know, the first eighteen years of life are the crucial years for achieving improvement in the muscular functioning of the body. After physical maturity is reached, much less can be done. This places on the shoulders of parents of handicapped children a heavy responsibility. Such parents have many special responsibilities, in addition to those carried by all parents. Among these special responsibilities is the knowledge that what they do now to improve the physical condition of their youngster may significantly influence the degree of handicap with which he will have to live for the rest of his life. Such a responsibility is a very heavy emotional load for anyone to carry.

Aside from the emotional problems involved, the assessment of possible improvement is not a simple matter. Particularly in the case of cerebral palsy, the parents may be up against a very confusing array of symptoms. Because cerebral palsy is a condition of organic brain damage, the symptoms are extremely varied, depending upon the area of the brain that is affected. For example, different portions of the skeletal-muscular system may or may not be affected, there may or may not be a speech defect, and there may or may not be mental retardation. Parents are often confused because *their* cerebral palsied child has a condition which is very different from that of another cerebral palsied child they know.

This, however, is not a book about the different forms which cerebral palsy or any other handicap may take. Instead, it is a book written to help you to understand some of the emotional and psychological stresses that are unique to you as the parent of a handicapped child. It will also help you to understand some of the ways of dealing with these stresses. For understanding the physical nature of your child's condition, you are probably already in communication with the appropriate medical specialists. Your child's pediatrician and orthopedist have probably already referred you to physical therapists who supervise your child's physical exercises and to speech therapists who provide training in that area. However, in the course of cooperating with these specialists and implementing their recommendations, you have perhaps been troubled by your own emotions and by the emotional reactions of your child. This was true in the case of Lois and Gilbert.

In our initial interview, Gilbert described his son, Mark, as having "tremendous will power which he is channeling into resistance against physical therapy." With irritation, the father added, "Mark seems to be happy just the way he is," and then complained further that they had to "push, push, push." Lois explained how strongly motivated she would be if she were in Mark's condition, and expressed bewilderment that Mark was not trying harder for physical progress.

The frustration, irritation, and bewilderment of these parents was understandable. Because they cared deeply about their son and his future, they were very upset by his apparent lack of motivation for doing his exercises and improving his physical condition as much as possible. It is difficult for a child to look ahead and foresee the consequences of what he does or does not do. Yet, time lost in the early years of physical development can never be recouped. Mark was an intelligent boy and able to grasp the point. Nevertheless, all the efforts of his parents to motivate him seemed only to strengthen his stubborn unwillingness. What was the real problem?

As my thoughts turned to this question, I began to draw Lois and Gilbert out a bit about themselves. As they talked, it became apparent that they were both intensely serious and conscientious people who tried very hard to do the right thing and to master any obstacles that life presented. In appearance, Lois was a very calm, soft-spoken young woman, whose voice betrayed not a hint of the feelings she talked of having. She described herself as being "too emotional," but a psychologist would have described her as "over-controlled." It was as if one part of her held a whip over the other part and demanded that she behave in a very sedate and ladylike fashion, regardless of how she felt. She lived under a feeling of being compelled to conform to unrealistically high standards of propriety. This pattern, which we psychologists call "compulsive," was evident in her husband also. In Lois, the compulsive suppression of her emotions resulted in periodic emotional eruptions, in the same way that a covered pot of water kept too long over a hot burner will collect steam which blows off the lid. Lois would then feel extremely guilty and tighten the reins of her compulsive control of herself. At the same time, she would try to tighten her control over the behavior of her son. Inevitably, he would rebel. This kind of thing leads to a battle of wills in which no one can win. Since the battle of wills was focused primarily on the matter of Mark's physical therapy, the stakes were high.

It is a simple thing for a psychologist to explain to parents that their efforts to push their child toward some goal will only evoke and increase his resistance against the very thing they want him to do. It is easy for a psychologist to explain that the solution to the problem lies in permitting the emergence of the child's own motivation by taking the pressure off him. The psychologist can even give specific advice about how to do this. But it is neither simple nor easy for the parent to follow this advice. Parents usually find themselves unable to follow such advice even though they want to. Sometimes, they think they are following the advice, but they are not truly in tune with it and it backfires.

Fortunately, Lois was wise enough to realize that simple rules were not what she needed. She knew that she would have to achieve some understanding of the struggle that was going on between her and Mark, and she knew further that this struggle had something to do with her own way of functioning as a mother. Admirably, she wanted very much to achieve an objective perspective on her own maternal functioning. She wanted to be able to look at herself as a mother and see how her behavior was affecting Mark and how it might affect a possible second child. Speaking with a quiet self-restraint that concealed her deep feelings, Lois confided that it seemed unlikely that she and Gil would have more children of their own. They were considering adopting one; but, before doing this, she wanted to feel sure that she would be "a good mother."

With this purpose in mind, Lois joined my therapy group for parents of cerebral palsied children. Because of situational factors, Gilbert would be able to attend only the first few sessions, but the progress Lois was to achieve would spread its benefits over the entire family unit.

CHAPTER TWO

From Generation to Generation

It must be kept in mind that this book is about the problems of adjusting to a child's handicap *and* about the ways in which a parent might receive help in making this adjustment by participating in a therapy group with other parents with similar difficulties. Rather than merely discussing the ways in which you might receive help through a therapy group, I would like to share with you the experiences of some of the parents in my group, thus letting you see for yourself how it works. There is something mysterious about the whole process.

There is within each human being, it seems, some deep, innate capacity for psychological growth and development. Have you sometimes found that, just when you thought some problem in your life was really getting you down, you unexpectedly found a new strength within yourself for solving it? Everyone has, at one time or another, gone to bed at night struggling with an inner problem and feeling rather hopeless about it, only to awaken in the morning with a new perspective which enabled them to see the problem in a quite different way. I grant you that solving life's problems isn't always that easy. But you do have within yourself a capacity for meeting the challenges life brings you. Often, the first difficulty you encounter is to get this inner capacity going. The process is something like turning on the ignition to start your automobile. And this is what group therapy is all about.

"What does that have to do with my problem of a handicapped child?" you may be asking at this point. "My child's physical handicap is real! No amount of inner strength on my part is going to change that." You are quite right, but I am sure you have also found that the day-to-day problems of living with a handicapped child, caring for him, and raising him to maturity really test your inner strength and your problem-solving capacities. And your having picked up this book tells me that you want some help in gaining a fresh perspective on these problems.

The question now becomes: how can I best help you? People often think there should be a simple set of rules for bringing up a handicapped child. There should be a particular way to feel about his handicap, to plan his future, to manage his relationships with his brothers and sisters, and to cope with the curiosity of other children and of strangers. It would be wonderful if this were the case. Of course, when you think about it, nothing so complex can be governed by simple rules. If I were meeting with you face-to-face to help you with these problems, I would not just listen to you for a few moments as you tell me about them and then give you the answers. Rather, I would need time to get to know you as a person so that I could help you to grow into your own problem-solving capacities. It is a truism in psychology that what helps one person with a problem does not necessarily help another person with a similar problem. There are similarities among people, but there are also differences. And, in your struggles as the parent of a handicapped child, you must find the answers that are right for you and your child, even though they may not be right for someone else.

"Of what possible value can this book be to me?" you may then ask. "If you could not give me much direct advice even in a counseling situation, Dr. Heisler, how can you hope to help me with my problems through this book?"

The answer is that, through this book, you can learn about the experiences of other parents of handicapped children, and you will find much that is applicable to your own problems even though your way of working through the problem may be different. As you read, I hope you will also become more aware that problems are not always what they seem.

This was very much the case for Lois. In the group, she found herself talking about the difficulty she had had in accepting the circumstance of having a handicapped child. This is always a difficult hurdle to surmount, but the ten parents in the group varied widely in their ability to admit having these feelings. People often try to feel what they think they *should* feel and to cover up—even from their own awareness—what they really *do* feel. This may do much more harm than good, because the denied feelings go underground and may surface in destructive ways. One of the benefits of the group was that it enabled these parents to bring their hidden feelings out into the light of day. The disclosures of one parent made it easier for another to reveal feelings he had never before talked about. For Lois and another mother, Jean, it was comforting to find that both of them had discovered their own nonaccepting feelings in the same way. For both of them, awareness of their lack of acceptance had first come through experiencing resentment toward childhood chums who had given birth to physically normal children.

Except for this brief excursion into exploration of her feelings, Lois spent most of the first three or four of the weekly sessions in silence, listening to the other parents. This does not mean that she was not involved nor was not a good participant. The ignition gets turned on for different people in different ways.

One of the things that can happen to a mother of a handicapped child is that she can get too intensely wrapped up in her child. This can readily happen to any mother for whom a particular child is a special problem. The handicapped child lives closely with special problems, and so does his mother, so it is easy for her to become very preoccupied with them. The child with the problems can become very much the focus of his mother's attention, so that her psychic energies are very much bound up in the relationship with him. Sometimes this overinvolvement may block the healthy development of both parent and child.

Most mothers have some degree of difficulty in letting their children grow up. For the woman who enjoys motherhood, there is tremendous gratification in the closeness with her child and in the depth of her child's need for her. As the child develops, he becomes more independent and the ways in which he needs his mother change. Although throughout his childhood his parents remain the most important people in his life, he gradually becomes less and less centered in the relationship with his mother, and other people increase in their importance to him. Although the mother naturally takes pleasure in seeing her child grow and develop, she also finds it a little hard to let go. After all, this child came into being within her womb, and she has felt him to be a part of herself. The physical separation that took place at his birth has also been followed by a gradual psychological separation. When this psychological separation becomes more apparent through his increasing independence from her, she may feel threatened.

In the case of the physically handicapped child, these problems are intensified and complicated by his unusual degree of physical dependence. This is a matter which we will consider in more detail in a later chapter. At this point, we are concerned with just one aspect of it, which has relevance to Lois's progress in the therapy group: When a mother has an unresolved emotional insecurity, she may unconsciously handle it through becoming emotionally dependent on her child. That is, the child's dependence on her will become necessary to her for her own emotional balance. This had become true for Lois without her realizing it.

The strange and mysterious thing about group therapy is that it can change such an emotional pattern even without discussion of the matter. In the group meetings of the first four weeks, there had been no references to the problem of overinvolvement with the handicapped child or of emotional dependence on him. Yet, by the fourth week of therapy, Lois and her husband, Gilbert, had left for a week of vacation, and this was a marked departure from Lois's previous unwillingness to be separated from her son, Mark, even overnight. Clearly, the tight bonds of her struggle with her son were loosening. A similar loosening was occurring for Jean in her extremely close relationship with her little cerebral palsied daughter, Jenny. She and her husband, Paul, who was also a member of the group, were suddenly discussing the possibility of using a coming business trip of Paul's as a basis for a vacation week-end without the children.

In the fifth session, Lois confided to the group that, when she had telephoned home on the first day of the vacation, she had found it somewhat upsetting to learn that Mark and his baby-sitter were getting along very happily without her. She admitted that she found herself asking, "What's happened to my little boy?"

Jean said that she could discuss with great intellectual sophistication the fact that parents do their children an injustice by never leaving them, but she had to admit that she and Paul had never left theirs overnight. They were surprised to discover that Jenny looks forward to Monday night (group therapy night) as the time when her parents go out and the neighbor girl comes in. This represented a striking change from Jenny's previous pattern of creating a scene whenever they left. Jean described how terrible the break had been for both her and Jenny when she first left Jenny at the cerebral palsy nursery at the age of two. Jenny screamed, and Jean cried all the way home. Jean feels this agonizing separation was intensified by the fact that she and Jenny had spent much time isolated together on a snowbound hilltop during Jenny's first two years. Jenny is now five years old, but seems younger because of her limited speech and severe physical dependency. I remarked to the group that these conditions often feed into the need of parents to hold on to the child unduly.

Dan, another member of the group, told of how his wife had cried when the school bus for handicapped children had first picked up their little girl and she had left with no fuss or tears. Roberta, a mother who bends over backward to present herself as mature, said she would be very disappointed in her children if she felt they were going to miss her whenever she leaves. Gilbert, whose work necessitates his leaving town for periods of time, exclaimed that Mark's adaptations to his absences do not mean that Mark does not miss him, but that the boy is able to accept the temporary loss. Lois was now able to say that she and Gilbert had apparently reached the point of being able to realize that their son was capable of getting along without them for a while, and she felt that coming to group had enabled them to achieve this realization.

Implicit in Gilbert's reply to Roberta was the significant point that a parent's ability to accept some separateness between himself and his child does not mean a weakening of the affection between them. This whole problem area was emotionally charged for the group members, who became involved in an animated exchange of viewpoints. Roberta protested rather heatedly about the "complaining" that had been going on during the group sessions, and she insisted that parents have no choice but "to take it." Jean replied that they all had a right to use this therapy for releasing their feelings about themselves and their problems, and Lois supported her with the quiet statement that this was why she was there also. Lois then added that she now knows that when she screams at Mark it is because of dissatisfaction with herself, whereupon Roberta protested that she yells because of things her kids do.

"Don't you think there is more behind it?" Lois asked quietly. Her therapeutic progress was showing up in her increased ability to look squarely at her own functioning as a mother. The following week Lois stated that this had been a very important session for her. Very close to tears, she said that after the last week's session she had realized for the first time that all her life, and not just with her son, she had "wanted to be missed."

"I want so very much to be missed," she reemphasized. "All of a sudden it just came home, and it was the strangest thing, because for the first time I really felt like I felt this way completely without reason." Because her feelings were so deep and had involved so much pain, it was hard for her to put them into words, but her meaning was clear. What she was really saying was that she wanted to feel loved. When, during the vacation trip with her husband, she had telephoned home and had found that her arrangements for Mark's care were working out very well and that he was quite happy without her, she felt that the boy must not love her. But after the session the previous week, she realized that she had no reason to think that. She saw that he could grow in independence without losing his love for her. And she realized further that her own deep need for reassurance of love from her son indicated some problem in her.

The source of her problem was not apparent at that time. The group had responded to her disclosure with further exploration of their own feelings about their children growing up, and in this context, Roberta "confessed" that she looks forward to the day when her children will be independent of her. Lois agreed that "this is what you raise them for—so they can have a life of their own," but she added that "you want them to be able to turn around as they go and look at you with respect and love." Self-exploration in future sessions would reveal to Lois that the source of her problem lay in the fact that her own departure into adult life had not been that smooth.

The thread of Lois's therapeutic work became temporarily invisible as the group focused on other matters, but it reemerged at a later point as she talked about feeling that she had always received less parental approval than had her brother and sister. The real break with her parents had come when Lois graduated from high school and wanted to leave home and achieve independence through a job. Her parents could not understand this need; they seemed unable to provide her with love if she were going to live outside the sphere of their control. Remaining true to her own need for independence, Lois left home; but, in so doing, she had to sacrifice the bond of family security. There were times when she longed to return to the security of home, but she felt there was little personal identity for her there. I associated this partial alienation from her parents with the intensity of her need to be loved by her son, and Lois was able to see the connection.

Another group member, Bernice, had a contrasting situation. Her parents lived near her and were actively involved in her family life. While she liked having her load eased by her parents, she had difficulty handling her feelings of obligation to them, and was frequently bothered by her feelings of resentment toward them. Lois, on the other hand, expressed resentment that help had never been available to her from her mother. Last year, following Lois's miscarriage, her mother "just happened to come out" with a friend, and she made a comment to the friend that had been very hurtful to Lois. She said that, had Lois needed her at the time of her miscarriage, she would have been unable to come because her other daughter was "expecting." In relating this incident, Lois exclaimed with feeling that her sister lives close to many other relatives and in-laws and also that she had had her husband with her, whereas Lois's husband had to be out of the country at the time and she was relatively alone.

"I occasionally think, 'What am I?' " Lois exclaimed. "I just don't understand it. I'd like to know what I did!"

Lois's release of painful feelings and resentment toward her mother was a necessary step in her personal growth and working-through of the problem which had brought her for help. However, such feelings cannot be brought to light without a reaction afterwards, and the following week she was suffering guilt over having "presented a harsh picture" of her mother. The tie-in between this problem and her battle of wills with her son, Mark, was becoming more apparent. Along with feeling guilty about her resentment of her mother, she was again tightening her control of Mark. That is, she was trying to tighten this control and was feeling frustrated that she could not. During the eighth session, she was very critical of her son.

"After an entire day with my son, I could tear my hair out," she stated in her incongruously quiet and well-modulated voice. She is particularly bothered that he is "uninhibited" and that she cannot predict his behavior in public. Calling upon Jean for support of her view, Lois was chagrined to find that Jean views Mark's behavior as "just being a seven-year-old boy." Jean told how embarrassed Lois was, during Jean's visit to Lois's home, when Mark asked for the cherry on Jean's ice cream.

"I admit this isn't the kind of thing you'd want him to do at the White House," said Jean, "but it really didn't bother me." Another example Jean gave of Lois's overreaction involved the time that Jenny had taken Mark some stamps. As the children were looking through his stamp collection, Mark exclaimed, "Oh, I've already got this one!" Again Lois was upset by Mark's freedom of expression. Lois could not agree that she was being unduly strict, and she tried to give the group a more convincing picture of Mark's misbehavior by telling of an incident in which he angered the school bus driver by his unruly play with some other children. In punishment, she took away his TV privileges and his allowance for two weeks and told him that, "if this doesn't work, I'll have to think of something to add to it."

She said to the group, "I've tried every conceivable way to bring him into line. What do I do?"

"Do you think he could be reacting to your own disapproval

of some of these small things?" asked Steve, who went on to tell of a time when helpful criticism from a friend made him and his wife Sylvia realize that they were worrying too much about small things. He wondered if this could also be true of Lois. The other members chimed in with material about their own children, trying to help Lois to see her own overreaction, and I again pointed out the danger that parental overcontrol may lead to a damaging battle of wills in which no one can win.

By this time, Lois was deeper into the experiencing of her mixed feelings toward both her son and her mother, and her motivation for the therapeutic work had strengthened. In a subsequent telephone call, she said that she was becoming aware of how much she "covers up" during the group sessions, but she guessed that the important thing was that after each session, she could face more squarely some of the things she could not admit during group sessions. She was now finding it very helpful to write out her thoughts and feelings, and she wondered if she could see me occasionally for private consultations. I agreed to this, and in these private sessions we explored some of her dreams, which were helping her to become more conscious of her deeper feelings.

During the following weeks, Lois also continued working with other members of the group on both her problem and theirs. The ninth session was an exceedingly full one, well-used by several of the group members. During one part of it, Lois was struggling with her confusion about how to view her mother, whose rejecting behavior toward her she had described in several incidents. To relieve her sense of confusion, I gave her my opinion that her mother really *is* unconsciously rejecting and hurtful toward her. Lois responded with a burst of emotion, expressing her deep sense of relief that someone else shared a perception which she had been almost afraid to admit.

"At least," asserted Lois, "it has given me some peace this last week just realizing and saying to myself, 'I don't love my mother, so what of it!'" This frank disclosure was upsetting to Bernice, who protested that mothers and daughters aren't always "chummy-chummy," but that one simply *does* love one's mother. When I pointed out to Bernice how bothered she was, she said, "Well, I'm afraid my kids aren't going to like me."

"This is really what has been bothering me, too," exclaimed Lois, who then turned to me and asked if her problem with her mother and her problem with her son were not related. I said that they were indeed. Lois then said, "It all seems to fall into place. I'm afraid that I'm rejecting Mark in the same way that my mother rejected me."

Bernice followed up on Lois's new-found capacity for insight by saying, "I'm going to give you some unsolicited advice. I've been thinking about your taking all that allowance away from Mark for that length of time for causing some trouble on the bus, and I thought it was pretty severe punishment!"

During the eleventh session, Lois talked further of her own struggles toward maturity. She said that, in leaving home, she had not really left her problems behind her as she had thought, but had merely buried them temporarily. While working and independent, she gained self-confidence. When she and Gilbert had met, she had appeared to him to be a very confident person. The recurrence of her emotional problems after marriage developed out of an unwanted pregnancy, upsetting their plans to wait two years before starting their family. In her quiet and carefully modulated voice, she went on to say, "I lost the baby," and then she added, "The shock of losing the first baby gave me a feeling of guilt because I hadn't wanted him." She now realized that her insistence upon having a second baby right away was motivated by the need to relieve her feeling of guilt. The second baby was Mark, and she had often wondered in what ways he may have been affected by all of this. Her anxiety that Mark might show severe adjustment problems now came out more clearly, and I gave the realistic reassurance that Mark's behavior, as described by her, did not warrant such concern.

Lois came to the twelfth session very much upset by a letter which she had received from her mother. The letter had been written after her mother had returned home from a visit with a friend who lived in the same general geographic area as Lois. Although her mother had traveled a long distance to visit the friend, she had not even telephoned Lois while there. Lois was again deeply hurt and angry. In what were (for her) unusually loud and vociferous tones, she exclaimed, "I went over and I sat down and I wrote her the most furious letter!'" Having thus vented her feelings on paper, she decided that nothing would be gained by sending the letter and that she would instead try to talk with her mother about their problem.

Lois told the group about the long telephone conversation in which she had tried to reach an understanding with her mother. Her attempts to convey how rejected she had felt met with evasiveness by her mother, who was apparently unable to enter into honest communication about the problem in their relationship. Through this telephone call, Lois began to develop some perspective on her mother's emotional limitations. It occurred to her that her mother had a problem of self-rejection and that this might underlie her rejection of Lois as an extension of herself. Lois remembered also that her mother had gone through something very similar to this in her own period of growing up. That problems of emotional adjustment can thus be transmitted from generation to generation suddenly became very real to Lois.

In the weeks that followed, she began to feel a new sense of inner strength. She had gained important insight into the fact that her relationship with her son was being affected by tensions carried over within her from past problems with her mother. These insights had a freeing effect on her, and she reported to the group, "I find I'm not nearly so bad tempered. I'm not flying off the handle so much. Painful though it is to think about these things, it seems to be relieving my tension." For the first time, she felt secure enough to admit that there had also been problems in her relationship with her husband. She had been a nag toward Gilbert, but she now felt that she would be able to change this pattern when he returned.

In a still later session, Lois talked of how difficult it had always been for her to assert her wishes or to let off steam. In her marriage, this pattern had combined with her husband's characteristic reserve to produce a minimum of spontaneous communication between them. For the first time, she talked with the group about how lonely she is during the periods when her husband has to be away. As her tears began to flow, her old pattern of overcontrol came up and she apologetically tried to stifle them. Everyone present supported her in releasing her lonely feelings; and, as she did so, the supportive sympathy of the group enfolded her like a symbolic mother.

As the ten-month series of therapy sessions neared its end, Lois brought the news that she would be unable to return next fall because of Gil's transfer to another geographic area. Their relationship had seemed much more full of joy since his return this time, and she also brought the good news that she was pregnant. She and Gil were hopeful that she might be able to reverse her pattern of miscarriages, for she now felt ready for pregnancy in a way that she never had before. [I later learned through follow-up communication that the pregnancy had indeed gone well, and that Lois and Gilbert were the happy parents of a healthy baby girl.]

In the last session of the series, Lois said in her soft and plaintive tones, "I want to say something. I told Verda some time ago that when I started this group, I think I knew in my heart that, for me, it was something I had to do because it very frankly meant my life. It has given me a great deal." Breaking off for a moment because of tears, she then went on, "The help I have received has made it possible for my family and me to live a better life. And that's what I wanted to say."

CHAPTER THREE

One of Life's Special Challenges

As the parent of a handicapped child, you have been presented with one of life's special challenges. Parenthood in general is one of the most basic and most important of all human functions. As a parent, you carry primary responsibility for your child's physical and emotional needs. No one knows better than you what a demanding responsibility this is. Being a parent not only consumes your time and energy, but it also reaches into your emotional life in a very compelling way. Everything that you are as a person finds expression in some way in your relationships with your children and in your ways of bringing them up.

All of this adds up to the fact that, while parenthood may bring joy and fulfillment, it also inevitably brings problems and emotional stress. For the parent of today, the stresses are compounded by the common knowledge that the early years are the formative years for the child's personality. Parents today are often afraid to be themselves with their children because of overconcern about psychological damage they may cause. Parental guilt feelings and fear of being blamed have become almost national ailments. This is too bad, because the advances in psychology can be a real source of help to parents when used in a constructive way.

If psychology is to be of help to you with either your handicapped or your nonhandicapped child, it must be used in a way that recognizes your individuality and the individuality of your child. This is often overlooked by parents who turn to numerous magazine articles on child-rearing for rules about "the right way" to handle a problem. Too often, a mother will try blindly to apply a generality which she has read without stopping to examine how she really feels about it or whether it fits her case. Although psychology has established certain basic principles that are true for everyone, they are true in different ways, for the human being is exceedingly complex and no two people are exactly alike. Just as a medical doctor cannot prescribe treatment for an ailment without first diagnosing what the ailment is, so also is it true that knowledge of psychology can be of help to you in your family problems only if used in a way that uncovers and clarifies the true nature of the problem. And this is just as true of adjustment to physical handicap as to any other kind of family problem.

"But the problem with my physically handicapped child is perfectly clear!" you may protest. "He just doesn't want to do his exercises. I only need to have you tell me what to do to handle this."

In the first two chapters, the fact that such a problem may indeed be more complicated than it seems was graphically illustrated. Lois and Gilbert came for help with their problem of a cerebral palsied son who was in rebellion against taking the exercises that were absolutely necessary for his physical improvement. Certainly, no one could say that they were "wrong" in being concerned about this and in wanting to impose their will upon him for his own good. Certainly, they would have been worse than negligent to sit by and let Mark waste the precious childhood years when some degree of physical improvement was possible. And yet, what would have happened if we had taken the problem at face value and had focused our attention on Mark's rebellion? What would have happened if I had been content to give advice, such as how to discipline Mark more effectively or how to make his physical therapy more appealing to him or how to reward him for trying harder? The chances are that the problem would have been intensified.

The reason that the problem would have been intensified by such an approach is that there was already too much attention being concentrated on Mark. Upset feelings were alive inside of Lois, and these upset feelings were demanding her attention. But she was not consciously aware of what the feelings were about, and unconsciously she was channeling the upset feelings into her relationship with Mark and focusing her attention on him. In this way, her feelings had an outlet, but they also had bad results—they were affecting Mark in a way that stimulated him to rebellion. Any physically handicapped child may rebel a little bit from time to time against the effort and monotony of physical therapy. But between Mark and his mother, a battle of wills was developing, and this gave Lois a new problem, in addition to the one which had been stirring around unconsciously inside her.

Are you bothered by my references to the unconscious? Although it is common knowledge today that much of what we feel and do and believe comes from sources within us of which we are not consciously aware, we often do not want to admit that we are not in full conscious control of our motivations and actions. Such unwillingness to admit the reality of our unconscious is too bad, because it prevents us from expanding our conscious awareness. As long as I refuse to admit that my unconscious exists, I make no effort to open it up and I remain at about the same level of awareness. When I become able to accept the fact of my unconscious mind, I also become motivated to explore it and to bring more of my own motivation into the realm of conscious awareness. As a result, I grow and develop as a person and become better able to cope with life's problems.

This is what Lois and some of the other members of my therapy group were doing. Lois had, of course, realized that she had a problem in her relationship with her mother, but she was not conscious of how much it was affecting her everyday actions. She certainly was not conscious of how her unresolved problem with her mother was feeding into a growing problem with her son. Only gradually did she become conscious of some of her own feelings toward her mother. As she did become conscious of her own hurt and anger, and as she achieved release of these feelings verbally during the group sessions, the pressure of her attention on Mark dwindled and he also was more free to be himself. And Lois discovered, to her amazement, that Mark's resistance against exercising had disappeared and the chronic tension was gone from their relationship.

As the parent of a handicapped child, you may now be saying to me, "But all of this applies just as much to the ordinary problems of rearing a nonhandicapped child. Because my child is handicapped, we have *special* problems, and I want some help with them!"

Quite true, on *both* counts. Let me respond to these two points in reverse order. It is very true that you are confronted with many problems not met by parents whose children are not handicapped. The life adjustment of your child is complicated and made more difficult by his handicap, and you are therefore called upon to be a source of emotional strength and sustenance for him in many special ways. Your patience and endurance, to say nothing of your energy, are strained by the unending, daily tasks of physical care. While the bathing, dressing, and feeding of an infant or young child may be a joyous activity for the young mother looking forward to the years of normal, healthy physical development ahead for her offspring, these same activities become less joyous and more burdensome when they continue into the years of middle childhood and when the prospects for the child's physical improvement are uncertain or dim.

Further drains on your time and energy come as you bend every effort toward utilizing the medical and community resources available for evaluating and working with your child's disability. On several days each week you may be involved in taking your child for physical therapy at one hour and for speech therapy at another. There may be visits to the orthopedic shop and many hours given to problems of brace-fitting and the subsequent adjustment of the child to the use of orthopedic appliances. You may have soul-searing decisions to make regarding surgery.

The whole realm of your child's social and educational adjustment may loom up before you full of frightening problems. You may have found yourself upset by the curiosity of strangers about your child's condition, and you may be worried about whether others will find him socially acceptable. Because of his limitations, you may have to make special arrangements for his activities with peers, and his education may confront you with many special problems. Always ahead in the distance is a big question mark regarding his future, his life adjustment as an adult. How much self-sufficiency will be possible for him? How can you best facilitate the optimal development of his capacities? If your child is one whose physical impairment is severe or whose problem is also complicated by mental deficiency, you may be worrying about how to work out provisions for his care during those later years when you will no longer be with him. You may even be confronted with the awesome responsibility of decision about special placement or institutionalization.

Problems such as these reach into the very core of your being. They touch some of the deepest levels of your emotional life. When you become a parent, your inner sense of personal identity becomes intertwined with the identity of your offspring. You experience your child as an extension of your own self, and all the good and bad feelings that you have about yourself and your life come into play in some way in your feelings about your child. You respond to him as a receptacle for your hopes, fears, and dreams. It is natural and healthy for expectant parents to look forward to the newborn offspring as one who will reflect the best of themselves. It is also natural for parents to fear that, in the years ahead, the child may reflect life tendencies which they dislike. And it is quite natural and not uncommon for parents to hope that their children will go further and get more out of life than they themselves have.

In the ordinary course of events, it is not a natural thing for parents to be emotionally prepared for the advent of a physically handicapped child. Most parents are quite unprepared for the emotional shock of realizing that their child is going to live with a handicap which will limit in unusual ways the life activities available to him and which will necessitate unusual expenditures of effort both by him and by them in order for him to realize the optimal fulfillment of his capabilities. Initially, in fact, most parents are not even able to realize that this is what the handicap means. Such realizations come only gradually and out of painful experience.

Painful emotional experience is inevitable for the handicapped child and for those who care about him. For the parent, the first pain comes in the recognition that the handicap exists. This recognition may be sudden or gradual, depending upon the exact nature of the handicap, its cause, and onset. In some cases, the child's defects are apparent to the physician at birth, and the physician informs the parents. More often, the impairment is not observable at birth and becomes apparent through the fact that the child's development does not proceed normally. In still other cases, a child is physically and mentally normal at birth, but later suffers an impairment as a result of accident or illness. Almost always—even in those conditions apparent at birth—the degree of severity of the impairment cannot be ascertained immediately. This element of unpredictability complicates the problem of accepting the reality of the handicap. It is very painful for parents to have to accept such a reality, and the pain is not reduced by the lack of definition of just what the reality is.

Any reader who finds this difficult to understand need only think of some time at which he has been in suspense over the possible occurrence of something which he dreads. As long as there is a chance that the dreaded thing will not happen, the person clings to hope that it will not, and acceptance cannot be achieved. In some situations, this is constructive, for hope will carry the person through the ordeal of being in suspense. And being in suspense for a prolonged period of time is indeed an ordeal. The acceptance of an established reality always brings a certain quality of relief. Once the nature of the child's handicap has been established and the reality of it has been accepted by the parents, they are free to move on to the task of working with this reality, unwelcome though it may be, in ways beneficial to their child.

However, in most cases, the process of establishing the extent of the handicap and the possibilities for improvement goes on over many years, and both the child and his parents are involved in a long and arduous process of testing these realities in order to determine what they are. Any challenge which life brings is a two-sided coin, carrying the possibilities of either psychological growth and development of the person or a sense of defeat. The challenge we have been discussing, of living with a handicap and testing out its reality over a long period of time, can have the constructive effect of sharpening a person's sense of reality, his ability to differentiate between the real and the unreal. It can, however, work in the opposite direction, bringing out the person's tendencies toward wishful thinking. This may bring a greater disappointment when the problem turns out to be worse than was expected. If the person cannot tolerate this disappointment, he may then be unable to accept the reality of the situation.

As the parent of a handicapped child, you have been confronted with the challenge of accepting an unwelcome reality. In a later chapter, we shall explore some aspects of this problem in further detail. At this point, however, I want to get across a particular message that relates more directly to what we were talking about at the beginning of the chapter. We have been discussing the fact that no two people will react to a problem in exactly the same way. In Lois's case, for example, it was obviously necessary to understand her as a person in order to help her with her problem with her handicapped son. We noted that this is generally true of the application of psychology as a helping profession, that harm can come from trying blindly to follow psychological "rules" or principles without thinking about just how and whether they apply in a particular case. You must recognize that you are a person first, and the parent of a handicapped child second; in other words, how well you do in meeting the special difficulties that come to you as the parent of a handicapped child will depend on the kind of person you are and how well you are able to face life in general.

It is natural and healthy for a person to seek as much happiness and enjoyment of life as he can find. But if you can be happy only when you have life exactly on your own terms, you are at a disadvantage. It is natural and healthy to want to invest your time and energies in activities that you like and find rewarding. But if you do not like to expend effort and if you do not want responsibilities that tax you, you will be able to give to life in only limited and mediocre ways. It is a natural instinctual response to avoid pain, and a human being thus tends instinctively to protect himself from sorrow and suffering. But if you must turn away from sorrow or unhappiness and *deny its existence*, you are weakening yourself by your own self-protectiveness and you are limiting your life to a superficial level at which you will have less to contribute back into the stream of life. It is natural and healthy to want to feel good about yourself and to accept yourself as you are. But if you can accept yourself and like yourself only by closing your eyes to your own weaknesses and adjustment problems, then you are not achieving true self-acceptance and you are limiting your own growth and development as a person.

What you are as a person is expressed in your relationships with other people. This is particularly true in your deeper and more intimate relationships. In your relationships with your children, this is true in ways that affect them deeply because their personalities are still in an early formative stage. As a parent, you are challenged to become the best person that you are potentially capable of being. This is the best gift you can bring to your child because what you are will affect him more than what you do.

As a parent, you live very much in a giving role. As the parent of a handicapped child, you find yourself called upon to give in special ways. Much of this special giving centers around the child's physical needs, and his emotional needs may therefore be overlooked. As I talk with you through the medium of this book, you will find that my overriding concern is for the emotional needs of your handicapped child. The importance of these needs cannot be overemphasized.

Concern for the child's emotional needs is concern for the child as a person. His development as a person will be of crucial importance for his future productivity and fulfillment. Even more than you, he lives confronted by the challenge of his handicap. He is the one person who has been confronted by this special challenge even more directly and completely than you have. In his living, he must meet the test of developing his potential as a person within the framework of limitations imposed by his handicap. Your support and recognition of him in his struggle will be one of the most important gifts you can provide.

CHAPTER FOUR

Is Your Handicapped Child Really Different?

"Well, I didn't feel that my husband was sharing—that he was doing his part in bearing the burdens, and I felt very hostile toward Doris because it seemed to me that she was keeping me from enjoying my other children as much as I wanted to." The petite young mother speaking with such admirable frankness was disclosing to the other group members some of the story of her long struggle toward acceptance of the blow life had dealt her. Her oldest daughter, now ten years old, wore a full set of braces and was able to walk only with the aid of a tripod. Her right arm and hand were also seriously affected, and the enunciation of words was still difficult for her. As she got older, Doris's inability to keep up with the activities of her two younger sisters had become more obvious, and her increasing obesity had also limited what her mother could do with her.

"I was always having to forsake them to take care of her, and I didn't like this," Jill continued. "I was taking it out on her, really. In the beginning I started out real concerned about Doris and I was going to do everything I could to keep her happy, and one day it dawned on me that by doing this I was neglecting my other children, so I talked with myself and decided that I would have to live for them as well as for Doris, but then I went through this period of hostility toward her. There was a confusing period when I could never make a decision. If my two normal children wanted to go with me someplace, it wasn't convenient to take Doris. I didn't have the time to load her into the car and unload her, you know. And I used to make them stay home because Doris had to stay. And that one time is all it took—that one time to take those two children with me—to leave her there crying with her Dad because I just couldn't forsake their lives. It seemed like she was controlling all of us and I just hated it. But it was just that one day that I really found the nerve to walk out on her—to leave her crying. And when we came back she was as happy as a lark. It bothered me more than it did her."

"It probably did her good," I told Jill, supporting the positive aspects of her functioning in this dilemma. "Because it really was a matter of your finding your strength to do the thing that was difficult to do because you felt guilty about doing it. And yet you recognized that it is not necessarily helpful to be overprotective with any child, handicapped or nonhandicapped. And you found the strength to do this thing decisively. I think this gives any child more security to know that there is strength in the parent. And your strength was not used cruelly, for the purpose of hurting her."

Jill agreed, explaining further that she had only gone to the laundromat for about twenty minutes and that it had been raining. But this incident was the turning point in her relationship with Doris, whom she subsequently became able to accept less resentfully.

The dilemma of conflicting feelings in which Jill had found herself to be caught was indeed a difficult one to resolve. There is never *one right way* in which any emotional conflict *should* be resolved, for the best resolution can only be that of which the person is capable at a particular stage of his own development. Emotional maturity, strength, and wisdom come only gradually, usually over the course of a lifetime. They are usually achieved through the process of facing problems and finding ways to cope with them.

It is very easy for resentment of a handicap to turn into resentment of the handicapped child. In a sense, it is the child who brings the problem to the parent. He does not do so of his own volition, and he suffers the burden of the handicap even more directly than does the parent. Still, he is the carrier of the problem, and it is natural for the parents to have feelings of wishing to be rid of the problem.

It is not only toward handicapped children that parents may have feelings of resentment, of course. It is natural, in the ups and downs of daily living, for feelings to fluctuate and occasional feelings of anger or resentment usually coexist with feelings of love. If a parent's feelings of resentment toward a child become frequent or intense or deep, the parent will probably tend to feel guilty about having these feelings and will tend to repress them. Whenever feelings are repressed, there is a tendency to act in an opposite manner. In this case, the parent's guilt feelings will be expressed through overprotection of the child. As if to prove his love for the child (to himself, actually), the parent will try to protect the child from any frustration or unhappiness. This deprives the child of the opportunity to find his own inner strength.

Since the advent of child psychology, parents have been confused about the matter of satisfying their child's emotional needs. They have been told that their child's future adjustment will depend largely on how well they satisfy the child's emotional needs during his formative years, but they haven't always understood just what these needs were or how they should be gratified. The most basic need of any child is, of course, for the security of being loved by his parents. Too often parents have taken this to mean that they should yield to every conscious wish of their child. Certainly, it is damaging to a child when parents are unnecessarily restrictive or prohibitive toward the child's conscious wishes. On the other hand, there are often sound reasons why a child cannot do what he wants and situations in which the child must accept frustration of his conscious wishes. This is not bad for the child because it gives him an opportunity to develop a tolerance for frustration, a very necessary attribute for anyone.

Frustration-tolerance is an important aspect of inner strength. Life brings some frustrations to all people, and the ability to tolerate them enables the person to make the most of his opportunities for development and fulfillment. One of my patients recently asked me, "Why is it that some people seem to grow and develop in strength as a result of their problems or misfortunes, while others are just crushed by them?" It is not easy to give a simple answer to this question, for many factors are involved. One important factor is this: the kind of inner adjustment a person makes to one experience of frustration will affect how well he is able to meet the next one.

When you are able to achieve acceptance within yourself of some frustration in your life, your acceptance of that reality will strengthen you and enable you to reach a more constructive solution to the problem than would be possible if you had not developed that frustration-tolerance. The inner strengthening will also enable you to meet subsequent problems more constructively. Thus, experiences of frustration may either strengthen or weaken a person, depending on what kind of adjustment he makes to them. This is as true for children as it is for adults. On the one hand, a child may be harmed by being subjected to more frustration than he can handle; on the other hand, he may be harmed by being so protected from experiencing frustration that he never develops inner means of coping with it.

Both of these conditions are weakening rather than strengthening to the inner child. It will be helpful to the parent to be guided by the goal of nurturing the child's inner strength. The parent will then be less tempted to restrict and frustrate the child unnecessarily, but will also be aware of the importance of helping the child to accept the frustrations that are intrinsic for him in a situation. Many of the minor frustrations in a child's daily living are softened for him by the knowledge that his parents love him and are motivated by concern for his welfare when, for example, they frustrate his wish to stay up when it is time for him to go to bed. But in the case of more serious frustration of deeper emotional needs, the child may need to be given some special attention and help toward gaining emotional acceptance of the frustration.

For the handicapped child, one of the realities of life is the fact that he is subjected to certain special frustrations not experienced by other children. Depending upon the nature and severity of his handicap, he may be frustrated in many of his natural needs for motor activity and the fun of physical play, for normal mastery of his physical environment, and for many kinds of self-expression.

Life confronts him with the necessity for developing a high level of frustration-tolerance, but this inner development does not occur automatically. As his parent, you do not really have the power to *shield* him from the frustrations inherent in being handicapped, but you are able to help him *deal* with them and to aid him in his inner adjustment to his special problem.

One of the most important things you can give your handicapped child is your recognition and respect for him as the individual that he is. The recognition of a child's individuality is important in all child-rearing, and it usually occurs quite spontaneously in loving parents as they enjoy and appreciate their child's personality and his particular forms of self-expression. For the handicapped child, his avenues of self-expression may be more limited, and his handicap may stand between you and your appreciation of him as a person. At times you may forget to look beyond the handicap to the child.

You may even be *afraid* to look beyond the handicap to the inner child, because you will have to see his frustration and his pain, and this hurts you deeply. His handicap is visible and apparent, but his inner feelings about it are not, and it is easy for people around him to forget his inner world of feelings. When you do this, you also forget his capacities for inner development, and his inner achievements go unrecognized. Many of the most admirable achievements of the handicapped child tend to go unnoticed because they are *inner* achievements—of fortitude, patience, frustration-tolerance, of inner strength. Of course, it is possible that the handicapped child will not achieve these attributes. He may instead withdraw into a shell of bitterness, resentment, and envy. Or, even worse, he may lose the capacity for resentment and may retreat further into a shell of self-rejection. When this happens, it is because he has felt so completely alone with his inner unhappiness, his inner struggles.

Childhood is a time of physical activity. Because of this, a physical handicap inevitably brings some degree of social isolation. Because of this restriction of peer activities, the child's relationship with his parents has even more than ordinary importance to him. This is not to say that the parents should substitute for peers. To the extent that it is feasible, provisions should be made for the child's inclusion in peer activities. However, there are special ways in which the child will need recognition and understanding from you. You are in a position to be aware of him as a person who is coping with a special challenge. You are in a position to give him respect for his efforts as well as for his inner and outer achievements. Receiving this recognition and respect from you will enhance his self-respect and self-esteem and his self-concept as a person. This is important because life will demand from him a great deal of inner strength to compensate for his physical deficiencies.

There will also be times when your child will have special needs for your emotional support and understanding. In the case of Doris, one of these times characteristically seemed to be in the afternoon after she returned home from school. Jill confided to the group her concern about "keeping Doris active and interested in life" and added that when Doris arrives home from school, she is disinterested in any activity except watching television. Steve, one of the fathers in the group, said that this did not sound unusual, and Jill stressed the contrast with her two younger daughters who arrive home eager for outdoor play. She thought Doris might at least read a book or amuse herself with some game. I wondered if this might not be a time of depression for Doris, and Jill exclaimed, "Yes!" but did not seem to know what to do about it. I asked then whether Doris shows any need to be near her mother and in conversation with her at these times, and Jill explained that she is busy in the kitchen at this time of day preparing breakfast and lunch for her husband, who leaves for work in the late afternoon. Doris does want to sit in the kitchen and help, but she is in the way.

"She's right there and I have to go around her and I don't always have that much time or patience to let her stir the eggs while they're cooking or help out. Or make toast—she doesn't butter it fast enough. It gets cold, you know, and the butter doesn't melt, and so I really do—I would like to know what I can do for her."

I said that the thing Doris seems to need at these times seems to be the thing hardest for Jill to give, for Doris is apparently compensating for her inability to go out and play by wanting to share with her mother in the kitchen activities. I wondered if Jill could soften the butter in advance and let Doris make the toast while sitting where she would be less in the way. Jill admitted that this would be good for her, but added, "But I'm not always that patient to stand there and watch her take four times as long to do something as it takes me."

"It brings the reality of her handicap home to you very powerfully," I said, "and that might be depressing to you. But I guess that is part of love—to share depression too, isn't it?"

Daniel came into the discussion with a real interest in ascertaining whether Doris has sufficient hand movement to learn to knit and might sit with her mother in the kitchen and knit socks for her father. Jill protested that Doris would not go off by herself with such activities, whereupon Daniel reiterated, "She could sit in the kitchen where you are and still be near you and yet be occupied."

It seemed to be difficult for Jill to understand and accept the importance to Doris of emotional closeness and support from her mother. Jill herself had been sent into depression by the blow of having a handicapped child, and she was still struggling toward acceptance of the problems it brought her.

"Through prayer, I have received the grace to endure all that I could not endure before," she said. "I was so despondent all the time. I thought I was good material for a mental hospital. I was beside myself with this problem. The fear of it all grabbed hold of me and I didn't know how I could ever be quite normal. But through prayer all these things that were so difficult for me have just become minor daily tasks. Whereas before—like putting on her braces every morning—that was—to get up, and right away—that was what I had to do every morning—put on her braces, and this really bothered me! And I thought, 'This is going to go on for years and years and years. What's the use?' "

The mother of a handicapped child carries the double burden of coping with her own feelings about the handicap and also of helping the child to cope with similar feelings. In order to be of help to the child in this way, the mother must be sensitive to what the child is feeling and must be able to empathize with the child's emotional needs. Through her empathy—her ability to sense the needs of the child—the mother will find within herself an intuitive guide toward the sustaining help she is called upon to give. But such empathy for the feelings of the child may not come easily to the mother who herself feels overwhelmed. The child's emotional needs may become quite lost in the torrent of emotion that the mother is swept up by. It becomes important for the mother to sort out and work through her own emotional reactions, both for her own sake and for that of the child.

CHAPTER FIVE

The Pain of Empathy

Even among those parents who elect to enter a therapy group of the kind we have been discussing, there are some who are not ready to accept the importance of sorting out their own emotional reactions for the purpose of being freer to provide emotional support to the child. Not only is this aspect of the therapeutic process painful, but empathy for the feelings of the handicapped child is itself a painful experience which the parent may unconsciously want to avoid.

Jean did not attempt to shield herself from the pain of empathy. She intuitively recognized that her warm support and closeness to Jenny would provide the child with a foundation of emotional security necessary for building the inner strength that would be needed so much in the years ahead. Almost five years old at the time her parents joined my therapy group, Jenny was described on her mother's application as "bright with an appealing personality. She is paraplegic, athetoid, and severely involved with cerebral palsy. She progresses steadily but still does not sit alone, stand, walk, feed herself, use her hands to any extent, or speak understandably. I understand her most of the time. She is very persistent in most tasks, curious, cooperative, willing to work at her exercises, a great teaser, amuses herself well, gregarious, likes to help with chores, healthy, attractive, seems happy. She has never mentioned or questioned her CP although I feel certain she must be aware of her differences."

The appreciation of Jenny as a person which shone through Jean's description of her on the application form was further apparent as Jean and her husband, Paul, talked with me in their initial interview about their wish to participate in the therapy group. At the same time, Jean made no attempt to hide her disturbed feelings about the physical and emotional burden that Jenny's handicap presents. For two or three years, Jean had been experiencing increasing difficulty in maintaining emotional control; and, more and more often, she was having what she called "my CP days" in which she found herself overcome by depression and hardly able to function. The fact that Jean referred to these low periods in her functioning as her "CP days" revealed that she unconsciously felt herself to be crippled by her emotions, just as Jenny was crippled by her cerebral palsy. The easiest solution might have been for her to try to shut out her disturbed emotions and rise above them. If she had used this defense, she would also have had to shut out her awareness of Jenny's suffering, and she would have lost her sensitivity to Jenny's emotional needs.

My reference to "Jenny's suffering" may come as somewhat of a shock, for there seems to be a common misconception that children do not suffer. This misconception may stem partially from the fact that a child's suffering may be less conscious and therefore less accessible to conscious formulation and clarification. Even in the case of adults, however, the conscious clarification of an emotional upset may be very difficult to achieve. A good deal of the work in psychotherapy goes toward achieving such clarification, which is valuable because the enlightenment of consciousness enables one to cope with one's emotions more constructively. Children usually do not have the advantage of highly developed conscious awareness in coping with their own unhappiness. They are therefore very dependent on the attitudes and emotional reactions of their parents. Too often, parents refuse to admit the reality of a child's unhappiness. They focus completely on the child's outer behavior and ignore the reality of the child's inner world of fantasy, feelings, and emotion. When this happens, the parent loses the opportunity for developing the kind of relationship in which the child would feel free to bring his parents his problems, express his feelings, or open up meaningful communication. As the years pass, the gap between the separate worlds of parent and offspring widens and becomes increasingly difficult to bridge.

The phenomenon of the "generation gap" is widely acknowledged today, although this aspect of its causation is not always understood. The parental tendency to overlook the child's inner world of feelings may often be more pronounced toward the handicapped child, because the parent unconsciously wants to avoid the pain of realizing the feelings of frustration, deprivation, and loneliness which are involved in the child's experiencing of his own handicap. Such awareness may stimulate the parent's own feelings of helplessness and depression about the problem. The attitude is widespread that such feelings should be suppressed because it isn't right to "feel sorry" for yourself.

Parents of handicapped children are often afraid that the child may feel sorry for himself because they think this will limit his ability to make a constructive adjustment to his handicap. They do not realize that it is harder for the child to come to a healthy acceptance of his handicap if he is required to stifle all of his unhappy feelings about it. Such suppression of feeling is particularly hard on the physically handicapped child because his outlets through physical activity are limited. He is left with no alternative but to withdraw into himself, and the irritated parent may then complain about his listlessness and apathy. It is much better for the child to feel the warmth and understanding of his parents' empathy for his unhappy feelings, even though this understanding may be put into words by the parents only at special times when the child is in particular need. Children are able to sense a great deal, and parental understanding is also communicated through the way in which problems are handled.

As Jean and Paul talked about their family life, the picture emerged of a happy home with lots of family activity and a developing companionship between Jenny and her younger sister, Sally. There were, however, increasingly frequent times when Jean was simply unable to maintain her good level of functioning because she was so overwhelmed by the pressure of her emotions. She welcomed the therapy group as an opportunity for catharsis of her pent-up feelings, which were released through tears during the initial interview and many subsequent group sessions. As she stated, she came with the goal of "working my upset feelings out of my system once and for all," and to this task she brought her valuable capacity for honesty and conscious awareness. In one of the sessions, when other group members were protesting against her tearfulness, she exclaimed, "We're sort of taught, or we read, that we're not supposed to feel sorry for ourselves. The world says you shouldn't; and, sometimes when I am, I say, 'I don't care, damn it! I'm not supposed to, but I *do* feel sorry for myself! I do! I do! I do!' God, I feel resentful sometimes that I'm in the position that I am!"

Because of her capacity to experience her resentment consciously and without self-deception, it was not misdirected to the child. Jean never forgot that the person who suffered the handicap most directly was Jenny, and her empathy for the child was deep and real. As she once said, "CP is a terrible crippler. Sometimes I can't stand it when the special nursery school bus drives out and I think about the kids in it—our Jenny included. They have such burdens to bear." She felt very keenly the pain which she knew lay ahead for her daughter, and she worried about being able to meet Jenny's needs at those times in the years ahead when Jenny would come to her with her suffering. I told Jean I sensed in her the capacity for giving Jenny what she would need most: namely, the sense of Jean's being with her in that suffering so that she would not feel so alone with it.

Receptive to my emotional support and that of the group, Jean made good progress. She shared with the group some memories of the unhappy period preceding Jenny's birth. A period of prolonged social isolation in an unfriendly community abroad had thrown her into a state of emotional withdrawal with severe hives. Following Jenny's birth, the gradual discovery of her cerebral palsy had been very traumatic, and Jean's self-confidence and sense of personal identity had been shaken. She came out of the experience feeling like "a has-been at thirty." It was as if life had passed her by and she would be unable to reestablish her place in the mainstream. Further social isolation awaited her after the return to America, for Paul's work took him to a remote New England community where Jean and Jenny spent much time alone during the snowbound winter months. It was during this period and later that the extent of Jenny's handicap was becoming known, and Jean and Paul were gradually achieving an emotional acceptance of the problem they would have to live with.

Acceptance of a handicap is not something that can be achieved once and for all. Rather, the road to such acceptance is a long and tortuous one, with many bends and turns, with many peaks and valleys. The fact that Jean and Paul had already traversed significant portions of this road was apparent in their ability to distinguish between Jenny and her handicap. Parents who have not yet achieved such acceptance will tend to identify the child with his handicap and reject the child as they reject his handicap. When the child manifests emotional problems, they tend to see the problem as a direct effect of the handicap. They often do not try to understand how the problem has arisen in the course of the child's experiences with his own handicap and his reactions to those experiences. This kind of confusion was visible in one of the mothers in the group who was disturbed by her handicapped daughter's brooding inactivity.

"Is this going to be the pattern of her life due to her handicap?" she asked me. To this mother, I tried to explain the importance of understanding her daughter as a person.

"I think her handicap has a great deal to do with her feelings," I said, "but she is a handicapped *person*. If you could understand her as the person that she is, and work at trying to understand her feelings and how she experiences her handicap and how she experiences life—how she experiences her relationship with you, and how she experiences her relationships with her father and her sisters, and what she really feels, and what's going on *within* her— through that understanding of her as a person you can best be of help to her. When you view it as if the handicap were the direct cause of her listlessness, you shut out any possibility of helping her with it."

To this, the mother replied that the handicap *must* be the cause of the listlessness, since her other two girls do not "act that way." This was an intelligent woman who was capable of comprehending the kind of distinction I was making, but she was blocked by her own unconscious feelings about the handicap and the difficulties it caused her. Before she could really provide emotional support to her daughter, she would have to go further in releasing her own disturbance about the problem in order to get perspective.

The ability to empathize with the pain of the handicapped child can, in some instances, cloud the issue of what is best for the child. In this situation, it is important for the parents to think the problem through as objectively as possible. Jean was trying to do this with regard to the problem of Jenny's night splints. Since the doctor had prescribed that Jenny wear them, the family had not had a good night's sleep. Jean finally went back to the orthopedist for explanation of the reason for the night splints, and he conceded that the needed protection of the hip sockets might be provided by Jenny's wearing the splints only until one A.M., at which time they could be removed. Even so, Jenny cried every night for two hours, and Jean turned to the group for help. She didn't know whether she could continue to endure "two hours of screeching every night," and she wanted help with evaluating the physical versus the psychological needs of the child. I asked Jean to clarify just what damage to Jenny's emotional development she feared. Not having thought of the problem in just that way, she found the question difficult to consider and answered by referring to other parents who had removed their child's night splints because "it was not worth the crying."

"It's having to cause pain that you don't want to accept, isn't that it?" Jean was asked by Steve, one of the fathers in the group.

"Maybe the mother gets more frustrated than the child does," added Dan, another group member.

I pointed out that, while it is difficult to make a choice between two evils, the child's frustration and discomfort may not produce psychological damage at all comparable to the physical damage that might result from not wearing the braces, since suffering unavoidable frustration and pain is not necessarily damaging to the child's inner development. Certain frustrations are intrinsic to physical handicap, and the crucial factor for the child's inner development will be the emotional climate in which he experiences these frustrations and the question of whether he is helped to tolerate them. I explained that the goal of developing the child's inner strength is not achieved through the elimination of all frustration and that, if Jenny had to live out her adult years with a severely impaired hip socket, she would look back with regret upon the fact that her parents had not done everything possible to alleviate the deformity.

"It helps me to hear you say that," said Jean, "because I don't think I ever understood that very well."

"When do you want to be hated, now or later?" asked Steve with ironic humor.

Paul then admitted that he is haunted by the thought that Jenny will some day ask whether her parents really did everything they could have when she was young. On the other hand, he knows that as parents they "get stretched to the breaking point."

Four weeks later, Jean brought the news that Jenny had been wearing her night splints with no further crying. However, the orthopedist had been so pleased with the results that he had now wanted her to wear them through the entire night, and this had precipitated another emotional crisis. Jenny had been helped to accept the splints by being told that, if she cooperated with wearing the splints until one o'clock, they would then be removed. Now, when the splints were not removed at that time, she cried until she fell asleep from exhaustion an hour-and-a-half later.

The various group members became actively involved in helping Jean to explore her conflicting emotions about the problem. She admitted that, on the second night, she had given in and removed the splints because she simply couldn't stand the sound of Jenny's discomfort. She felt deeply concerned about the condition of Jenny's hip socket, but she also felt utterly unable to subject her child to the severe discomfort which the child seemed unable to tolerate.

Since Jean continued to be unable to resolve her conflict, I made clear to her the distinction between two considerations which she was confusing: namely, that of possible emotional damage to Jenny through crying, and that of the parents' own level of tolerance. I suggested that she try to keep these separate in her thinking in order to be more objective in her evaluations.

"My own feeling about Jenny," I stated, "is that she is receiving the emotional support she needs for good emotional devel-

opment, and that she can be helped to tolerate this physical discomfort. I shudder when children, crippled or uncrippled, are
subjected to unnecessary frustrations and punishments and deprivations—frustrations that really serve no constructive purpose for
anybody. These are damaging and there is no justification for them
and they always bother me. But there *is* justification for this, if it
is really going to make a difference in her hip structure all the rest
of her life. This is now, and she can't appreciate that. A five-year-
old child simply doesn't have the mental maturity yet to evaluate
that and make a decision."

It was two months before the matter of Jenny's night splints
was next brought up. Jean and Paul brought the good news that,
since we had last talked about it, Jenny had worn the splints each
night until the prescribed four A.M. with no crying at all. Once the
mother had come to a genuine acceptance of the necessity for the
splints, she was able to be firm with the child in a loving way, and
this in turn enabled the child to accept and tolerate the discomfort.

Jean's resolution of her conflicting feelings about the night
splints was a manifestation of her therapeutic progress. Her progress was showing up in other ways also. To the group, she reported
that the periods of depression which she had labeled as her "CP
days" were disappearing. The liberation of her energy had made
possible her decision to return to part-time employment, and this
provided a welcome renewal of her sense of professional identity.
Such changes through psychotherapy are usually accompanied by
dreams, which reveal that the progress is rooted in a shifting of
deeper, unconscious patterns.

Dreams speak through the language of symbolism, which often
brings diverse facets of a psychological situation together through
a kind of shorthand. One of the dreams which Jean brought to the
group summarized in a compact way her sense of empathic identification with the handicapped child, her fear of getting lost in the
waters of her unconscious disturbance, her feelings of being helped
through the therapeutic relationship with me, and her motivation
for overcoming the obstacles which life might bring to her and
her handicapped child.

The group listened intently while Jean related her dream:
"A group of us were standing by a river talking, and suddenly you

[the author] jumped in the water. I sort of got excited, but your husband said, 'It's okay. She's a good swimmer.' And what had happened is that a child had fallen off the other side of the bank and you had noticed it. Probably I was so busy talking I wasn't aware of it, and you had jumped in to rescue him. It was a small boy, and his face was very clear, but I didn't recognize him at the time. It was a dark, swarthy kind of face, and I kept thinking about that face, thinking about that face, because it looked familiar, but I didn't know who it was. So then this was Tuesday morning and I had gone to work, and at nine-thirty Tuesday morning I was sitting there observing a student, and just like that it flashed through my mind that that face was Emik Avakian."

To the members of the group who did not know who Emik Avakian was, Jean explained that the local cerebral palsy agency had recently shown a documentary movie giving recognition to this severely handicapped man for his outstanding achievements in a scientific field. His scientific contributions were all the more impressive because he had achieved them despite the very severe impediments of his cerebral palsied condition.

In associating to the dream, Jean said, "I thought of you as a hero who was going to save us and save all the crippled children. Emik Avakian represents to me crippled children in general, I guess."

Bernice, another group member, commented, "The child could be an extension of someone needing help, not even a child perhaps." This comment opened up an important significance of the dream, for in dreams a child frequently comes up both as a symbol of the dreamer's need for help and of his potential for psychological growth and development. It made very good sense that, in Jean's dream, her potential for inner growth and development was symbolized by a handicapped child, for the way in which life had challenged her to grow was through the problem of her daughter's handicap.

Over the two-year span during which this therapy group functioned, Jean and Paul faced many painful aspects of Jenny's condition. Maintaining her supportive closeness to Jenny, Jean was aware of the child's growing realization of her difference from non-handicapped children. It was particularly hard for Jenny to watch her younger sister moving ahead of her in physical development and freedom of mobility. Jenny's inability to enunciate words clearly also interposed a difficult barrier between her and others in social communication, and this troubled Jean deeply. Despite these serious problems, Jenny manifested undeniably good personal and social development. Many incidents which Jean and Paul described to the group illustrated Jenny's ability to tolerate frustration and her keen and deep capacity for pleasure. The child seemed to exemplify the well-known psychological principle that the brightness and joy of life cannot be truly known without experiencing darkness and pain.

During the closing weeks before the termination of the group, Jean brought news that was both gratifying and frightening to her.

"I am living through days that I have dreaded for years," she said. In the past, Jenny had occasionally asked about her condition and had simply been told that she had cerebral palsy. Since she had not pursued the questioning, nothing further had been said to her in explanation. Now the time had come when she wanted to know what cerebral palsy is. Jean had known this time would eventually come, and she had feared that emotion would overpower her and make it impossible for her to answer Jenny's questions objectively. She was finding, however, that she was able to maintain her composure while giving Jenny a simple, factual explanation. Jenny also was remarkably objective in her approach but puzzled that damage to her head could affect her legs. It is understandable that a child of age six-and-one-half would be puzzled even by a greatly simplified explanation of the motor functioning of the human body. Yet, giving the answer in these terms helped to reinforce the attitude of objectivity with which she raised the questions.

Jenny, who was attending a special school for children with various kinds of handicaps, then proceeded to ask her mother which of the children at her school had cerebral palsy. Then, in each case, she asked about the cause. In this way, she led up to her final question about what had caused her CP. With some difficulty, Jean explained to Jenny that she had been injured at birth. Jenny concluded the inquiry by asking whether her mother would still be there when she was grown up.

When Jenny resumed her questioning some days later, her

focus had shifted to her own future potentialities. She asked such questions as "Will I walk?" and whether one could be a librarian in a wheelchair. From these questions, it was clear that already Jenny was looking ahead to her adult life and trying to assess the degree to which she would be capable of functioning independently and of contributing to her own support.

When parents ask me what they can do during the early years to make sure their handicapped child will become as self-supporting as possible in his adult life, I emphasize the fact that the child has a natural motivation toward independence and productivity which will find its own route for development if the child grows up with a sense of worth and self-esteem. Jenny was esteemed by her parents as a person worthy of their respect, appreciation, understanding and empathy. In the sunlight of these loving feelings and constructive attitudes toward her, she bloomed in the development of her capacities for initiative, courage, perseverance, and objective thinking about herself and her own special problem.

There is no doubt that, when Jenny reaches adulthood, she will find many difficulties in making a place for herself as a productive member of society. Some of these difficulties will stem directly from the structure of physical limitations imposed by her handicap and within which she must function. Other difficulties will stem from the attitudes of other people who, for a variety of reasons, will discourage her efforts and limit her opportunity to find ways of circumventing her handicap or compensating for it. Within the competitive, work-a-day world, there is great emphasis upon conformity for purposes of simplifying the complexities of modern living. A person who is "different" in a way that limits ability to conform introduces special problems and complications into an educational setting or a work setting which is geared to uniformity of physical functioning. For this reason, the handicapped person may not be welcomed, and his presence may even be opposed. In order to meet the challenge of such restrictive forces constructively, the handicapped person must possess a high level of self-esteem as well as courage, ingenuity, and fortitude. I believe that Jenny will have this inner strength and will succeed in becoming a contributing member of society because of the good psychological foundation laid down during her formative years.

CHAPTER SIX

Acceptance of Hopelessness

The group through which I worked with the parents of cerebral palsied children continued over a two-year span of time, interrupted by a three-month break during the summer months. When the coming of autumn brought resumption of the group, several people dropped out to make way for new participants, and the two couples who entered at this time had children whose handicaps presented special difficulties in acceptance.

Sometimes the impairment of a child's functioning is so severe both physically and mentally that, even with the passage of years, the child cannot develop beyond the level of infancy. The care required by such a child exceeds that needed by the usual infant because the physical and mental retardation is usually accompanied by special complications. As the years pass with no alleviation of this burden and with the permanence of the condition becoming more undeniably apparent, the parents find themselves forced to consider institutionalization for the child. This was the problem which confronted Pat and Brad, and the challenge to them was therefore different from those we have been discussing in preceding chapters. For them, the challenge was to reach acceptance of the hopelessness of their child's condition.

The fact that Pat and Brad had been able to maintain hope

over the four years of Bonnie's existence was indeed a tribute to their parental love, but the toll on them had been tremendous, and certain deprivations to Bonnie's five siblings had been unavoidable. Just a month before entering my group, Pat had conceded for the first time that the welfare of the total family might have precedence over her sense of responsibility to the retarded child, and Bonnie had been placed in a foster home with a woman who devoted her life to the care of a few children with such conditions. Pat had started working, both to help meet the expense of Bonnie's care and also to ease her own adjustment to the change in her life.

A small woman, whose delicate facial features and almost inaudible voice conveyed a sense of fragility, Pat expressed her doubt that the therapy group could be of help to them now that the problem had been solved. The placement of Bonnie had relieved the tension in the home, and Pat was not looking farther ahead at this time. Over the past four years, she had sustained herself emotionally by not facing the full import of the problem, and now she wanted to believe that the final resolution of the problem had already been achieved. More realistic than his wife—both in his appraisal of Bonnie's condition and of emotional factors in the family adjustment—Brad pointed out that the problems had not really leveled off but were only in a temporary lull.

One area of concern to him was the feelings of Bonnie's siblings about her removal from their home. Bonnie herself seemed to have such limited comprehension that her ability even to differentiate her parents from other people was in doubt. It was, however, hard for the other young children in the family to understand this, and Brad kept wondering how Bonnie's placement outside the home would affect the other children in the long run. He feared that they might develop guilt feelings as a result of the expansion of family recreational activities made possible by the removal of Bonnie from the home. This concern was most pronounced with regard to six-year-old Julie, who had been very involved with Bonnie as a new baby, but who had withdrawn from Bonnie because of her unresponsiveness and had transferred her attention to the next baby, now about a year old. Brad was looking forward to the opportunity to discuss these matters with other parents in the group.

During my initial session with this couple, Brad also brought out his hope that, through the group, Pat would be able to open up her feelings a bit more. As we have noted in the earlier chapters, people find various ways of protecting themselves from feelings they are afraid to experience. Pat's demeanor of extreme reserve had a self-protective quality which suggested the possibility that, during her earlier years, she had had an experience that in some way had driven her back into a shell that could be shattered by an approach that was too direct or assaultive. It was very much to her credit that, despite her vulnerabilities, she had carried unusually heavy family responsibilities very well for several years. During the first year of Bonnie's life, her parents took turns staying up with her all night in order to try to relieve her physical discomfort and crying. Because sucking and swallowing were so difficult for the baby, much time and patience were required for her feeding. Constipation was a regular problem, and enemas or suppositories were necessary to produce a bowel movement. Four years later when, through the support and encouragement of my group in its final months, these parents took their child to a clinic for evaluation relative to institutionalization, Bonnie still slept very poorly, required an hour for a feeding of baby food, and was unable to eliminate without an enema. Her additional orthopedic problems included partial blindness and spastic quadriplegia. And her mental level was below six months.

By the time Pat and Brad entered my group, Brad had begun to consider institutionalization. Over the years, he and Pat had taken Bonnie to many doctors and many clinics. Some of these had held out glimmerings of hope during the first year or so. For a long time, there had been no basis for hope in the medical prognoses, and yet Pat could not let go. She had kept herself functioning through a belief in the impossible, and it was difficult for her to relinquish that belief.

It would have been easier for me and the group members to help Pat if she had been able to release her sorrow and examine the realities of the problem within the understanding and comfortable atmosphere of group support. This is what her husband hoped for. But this was not Pat's way. It was as if she could handle her inner turmoil only by limiting the extent to which she faced the problem and her feelings about it. It was my hope that over the period of nine or ten months that she would have in the group, Pat would be able to expand her area of confrontation with the problem. Only in this way could she reach a decision that she and her family could live with.

During the first few weeks that Pat and Brad were in the group, Brad presented a realistic picture of Bonnie's condition and the attendant family pressures, thus trying to enlist the aid of the group in thinking through the question of whether to place Bonnie in a state hospital, at least for a trial period. The problem became even more immediate when Bonnie's placement in the foster home had to be terminated when the foster mother fell while carrying her and Bonnie's leg was broken. When Bonnie was released from the hospital, the foster mother would not take her back, and Brad took leave from his work to stay at home with the child until he could make further arrangements.

Since Pat continued to be almost silent and quite emotionally inaccessible in the group, I set up an individual appointment for her and saw her privately. At the beginning of the hour, I extended my sympathetic feeling, to which she responded with the admission that she did not know what to do and did not want to make a decision. As her focus seemed to be on the immediate problem of finding another foster home, I commented that they had two different decisions to make, not only that of immediate care for Bonnie but also the matter of long-range planning. Pat replied that she just wanted to postpone decisions but that Brad wanted her to make them.

As I talked with Pat about the fact that Brad wanted her to enter into the decision-making process because her feelings were involved, she opened up a bit about the family problems that have resulted from Bonnie's broken leg and about the difficulty in finding someone to care for her. Then, referring to the long-range problem for the first time, Pat stated that she and Brad had submitted an application to the appropriate state hospital and had learned that Bonnie could be accepted without delay. However, they were still hoping for Bonnie's admission for extended observation at an evaluation school to which they had applied a year ago.

Pat and I then talked about the group, and I asked whether

she thought it was going to be helpful to her. She replied that, in the beginning, she felt that her problem had dissolved and that the others had more to talk about. I pointed out quite directly that the problem of Bonnie's care had continued to exist, even though it had become less urgent, and that she apparently had many mixed feelings about this. I said that the group members and I wanted to help her to explore her mixed feelings about what to do about Bonnie, as we understood how very difficult this must be for her. With characteristic blandness, Pat replied that it is so much easier just to wait to see what tomorrow brings. After a moment of silence, she admitted that she fears the hurt of letting herself get too involved in the problem. I asked if she felt that, through coming to the group sessions, she might become better able to face the situation and to endure the feelings that might emerge. She replied that, if someone would just tell her that Bonnie will always be the same and will never improve, she could accept that. As her hopes seemed to be pinned on the evaluation school located in another city, I urged that she and Brad renew their efforts to get Bonnie admitted there for observation. As an alternative, though more limited, source of evaluation, I suggested the local child development center.

Approaching the subject with caution, I commented on how hard it must be on a mother to have this problem, but Pat redirected my comment back to the decision to be made. She said she did not really know what Brad wanted to do, because he wanted her to make the decision. I spoke of how their decision might be more easily reached if it evolved out of a process of talking about the problem and working through their feelings. Showing some emotion for the first time, Pat then described the long process of increasing realization of the nature and severity of Bonnie's impairment. She was also able to bring out her fear that the other group members might not be able to understand the special problem of Bonnie.

As we had then run out of time, I remarked that it must take courage to return to group, and Pat said that she gets something out of coming but fears having to talk. I asked if she preferred that I just wait until she herself begins to talk or whether she would like me to draw her out. From Pat's rather ambiguous answer, I sensed that she would experience such support as pressure, and would not want it.

In the next group session, I described the services of the local child development clinic, both for the benefit of Pat and Brad, and also for the other couple, Harriet and Randy, whose child presented some special problems that needed clarification (the latter problem will be discussed further in Chapter Seven). I explained that, prior to the clinic conference, various aspects of the child's functioning would be studied separately by various specialists, including a child psychologist, speech therapist, audiologist, and orthopedist. A public health nurse would visit the home to talk with the parents. On Clinic Day, these specialists would confer together with a pediatrician, presenting their findings to him. He would then examine the child. The parents, present throughout this conference, would then be given a recommendation based on this comprehensive evaluation.

I further explained that, on the Clinic Days scheduled for Bonnie and for Harriet's child Ernie, I would cancel my own office appointments in order to attend these conferences, as it would be helpful to me in working with these parents to have the exact realities of the child's condition as clearly defined as possible. Neither mother responded overtly to what I had said, but Brad stated that he would like to have this done, and asked when it might occur. I told him that the waiting period is usually about four months but that we would try to get this speeded up. The other father, Randy, asked whether the mental level and maximum possibility of the child would be ascertained, and I said this would be one of the goals of the evaluation.

In subsequent sessions, Pat began to open up a bit, repeating for the group some of the discussion that she and I had had privately. Through verbal admission of how hard it was for her to think about the problem, she gained the support of the group in trying to do so. With a little more freedom, she began to release some of her feelings about what a chore Bonnie's care had been, and then she admitted that she had known for a long time that Bonnie was too retarded to care who was looking after her, as long as she was made as comfortable as possible. During a session when Brad was absent, Pat confided to the group that whenever things start to go wrong Brad suggests that she quit her job and she has to convince him that this would not help matters, making her feel worse, instead. Dropping her guard even further, she remarked that she was always relieved when she could turn Bonnie's care over to Brad, but that she felt a little guilty about this.

In another session, Pat and Brad together talked about some of the sibling patterns within their family and the competing needs of their children, ages fourteen, ten, seven, five, four, and two. The emotional dilemma that having such a badly impaired sibling presents to children came out in Brad's description of their shifting reactions to Bonnie's presence and absence. When she was in their home, all the children had times of resenting her and not wanting her there; yet, they all had felt that her placement in the foster home was "not right." Harriet pointed out that Bonnie's placement must make the other children feel that they too could be "pushed out and taken back at will—that if Bonnie can go, they can go just as easily." Pat said she hadn't thought of that, and Brad said he supposed it could be true. Apparently needing more time to digest that thought by himself, he turned to a description of some of the problems they had suffered through with Bonnie, such as the period of her prolonged crying at night. The exact cause of the crying had never been determined, although she had been given much medical treatment to correct physiological deficiencies. Brad described how he would "cradle myself in a mattress between two walls of a corner of the room" in order to get some sleep while holding Bonnie in his arms at night. His longest period of uninterrupted sleep was seldom more than forty minutes. He joked that at his office he was regarded as a hyperactive individual because he couldn't stand still.

"They didn't know," he said, "that if I stopped moving I would go to sleep."

Pat and Brad received notification of the scheduling of Bonnie's Clinic Day at about the same time that her appointment for a two-week period at the evaluation school was set up. They decided to take advantage of both. Brad stated rather decisively that if no indications for Bonnie's future developmental progress could be found, he would favor placement, for the penalty that the entire family would have to pay by keeping her would be too great. Pat expressed concern about the tragedy of children who are institutionalized as hopeless when actually they have an unrecognized potential. I supported her need to be very sure of the facts of Bonnie's condition, and this enabled her to verbalize the other side of the coin that if she and Brad were told that Bonnie had some potential for learning, she did not know how they could find time to bring it out.

In the session following Bonnie's Clinic Day, Pat and Brad received interested questions from the group. Pat replied without apparent emotion that it had been determined that Bonnie could not be trained. Her language level was thought to be about six months. Jean asked Pat if they had discussed with the clinic staff their thought of institutionalizing Bonnie, and Pat replied that the clinic had recommended this and had offered help in doing it. The clinic staff had also informed them of other parents in this community who have placed children in the state hospital, and had encouraged them to contact these parents. I told the group of the recognition that had been given to Pat and Brad for the marvelous care they had given Bonnie. The statement had been made that it was almost miraculous for a child with Bonnie's degree of impairment to have survived, and that Bonnie was in remarkably good condition. In response to this, Pat spoke of the bad condition into which Bonnie would sometimes sink and of how hard they would work to bring her back again. I told these parents that, in placing Bonnie, they could certainly look back with the knowledge that they had done everything that could possibly be done.

Jean asked whether they had discussed with their other children their plan to place Bonnie. They felt the older children had some awareness of what was happening although it had not really been discussed. I suggested that the adjustment of the other children to Bonnie's institutional placement would probably be easier if they were brought in on the planning early and were given an opportunity to ask questions and express their feelings about it.

Following the period of observation of Bonnie at the evaluation school, the group was again interested in results. Pat, who had found it very interesting during her two-week live-in period to see how the school was run, gave an informative description of its population and policies, but thereby evaded the problem of Bonnie. Someone asked if Bonnie had been given a lot of tests, and Pat replied, "Well, a lot of people saw her." Asked more pointedly what had been decided about Bonnie, she said that Bonnie was not accepted to remain there because she was not trainable. I then asked if a recommendation had been made, and Pat answered that placement in the state hospital had again been recommended. I then asked if she felt any more prepared for doing that, and she said, "I guess I am, gradually."

Somewhat less taciturn, Brad detailed the prognosis they had received that Bonnie would never walk or talk, would never be able to sit up or feed herself. Remembering his own experience as a child with a long-unrecognized, serious visual defect and the great difference made to him by the prescription of glasses, he could not help hoping that visual aid to Bonnie would also bring other improvements, but he realized at the same time that whatever small improvements could be reached would probably make very little difference to Bonnie's pattern of life. Apparently having reached acceptance of the necessity for hospitalization, he tried to help Pat toward this, concluding, "If the time is not opportune now for placing her, it will never be opportune."

There was deep and prolonged silence as everyone pondered the gravity of the decision to be made. Eventually I asked, "How do you respond to that, Pat?" She replied that she knew that placement would only become more difficult with the passage of time, and she told, as she had in the past, how the family responsibilities leave so little time for the care Bonnie needs. I conveyed my own concern over the great toll taken on her and Brad, and my wish that they would permit themselves this relief.

Pat and Brad were somewhat bitter in their preoccupation with another child they had seen at the school who, while not much better than Bonnie, had been permitted to remain for prehospital training. This child apparently had more potential than had been developed by the parents, and I explained that this is a different matter from trying to develop more than exists. I brought Brad back to his earlier statement that the time had come for making a decision one way or the other. He replied that he would go further than this and say that the time had come for placement; but, that if such a decision could not be lived with, there was another alternative:

really deciding to keep Bonnie and to devote their lives to her care. "Let's go all the way," he finished. "Let's not dilly-dally in the middle of the stream."

"What you are saying," I told Brad, "is that if Pat can't live with the decision to hospitalize Bonnie, then rather than have Pat unhappy and guilt-ridden you would go along with the other decision, but you would like Pat to be decisive one way or the other." Pat then said that she would like to go up to the state hospital and take a tour of the entire place, and Brad agreed that they could go next Sunday or the Sunday after.

After a while, Brad pointed out that hospital placement is "not a finality," that Bonnie could be visited and also brought home for visits. If institutionalization should prove to be unsatisfactory, Bonnie could be removed. After another period of silence, I told Pat I felt she must have very upset feelings and that I would like her to try to express them. She did not reply, and I added: "It's hard to let go of a child to whom you have given birth." As Pat began quietly weeping, Brad remarked that to place Bonnie without emotional acceptance of doing so would result in other problems for the entire family. He felt that if Pat preferred to keep her at home, there were ways in which this could be worked out. He went into some detail about this, mentioning as one factor among several that it might be easier if Pat were to give up her job. He seemed to be trying not to subject Pat to pressure toward a decision in the direction he preferred.

During the next session, Jean commented that she couldn't help thinking about how nice Brad was in his approach to Pat, in being careful not to push her into a corner and in leaving her free to make her own decision. Harriet said it would perhaps be better if Brad would simply make the decision for both of them, and Pat replied that was what Brad did not want to do. She added that it would have been easier for her to give Bonnie up during those difficult first years, but that Brad would not consider placement until he had made a full try.

Brad had stayed away from this session, probably to give Pat an opportunity to explore her feelings with the group without his presence. While Pat still was not ready to commit herself to a decision, she seemed to be drifting toward hospital placement. I again stressed the importance of advance preparation of the children in case institutionalization were decided upon. Harriet asked if the children could not be taken to the hospital to see it. While Pat's initial reaction to this was negative, Jean said that she also had been thinking it would be helpful to the children to see the place to which Bonnie was going. I reinforced the point made by Harriet and Jean, explaining that by seeing the hospital, the children would know that Bonnie was at a real place. Without this concrete knowledge of where Bonnie was, her removal from the home could be a springboard for all sorts of unconscious fantasies.

"That she may have died," amplified Harriet, adding that under similar circumstances she would never again have trusted her parents. I mentioned having known several instances in which the mysterious disappearance of a pet had traumatized children, and this led immediately to relevant associations from everyone. The conversation seemed helpful to Pat, who agreed that the children could be included in trips to take Bonnie out of the hospital for a day.

Pat then talked about how difficult it had been to answer the questions of the older children about how much Bonnie will be able to do when she is older. I suggested that these questions also provide an opportunity for bringing the children into the planning for placement. Pat asked if it would not be too hard on the children to be told that Bonnie would remain at the hospital for the rest of her life, and I agreed that it was unnecessary to mention that aspect unless the children asked specifically about it.

The following week, Pat again came alone. I reopened the subject, for the end of the group sessions was drawing closer. Still indecisive, Pat said that she and Brad were going to revisit the hospital this week, but that no steps had been taken to prepare the other children for Bonnie's departure. Pat told of an incident in which she had asked two of the children to help her with Bonnie and they had protested. In that situation she had wanted to tell them that Bonnie would soon be gone, but she checked herself, realizing that telling them at such a time would arouse guilt feelings in them. The group supported Pat with recognition of her self-awareness, and then we talked about the fact that the children would need help in gradually becoming accustomed to the idea of Bonnie's placement, since, even for an adult, time is required to absorb the reality of the need for placement and to come to accept it.

In the next session, Pat and Brad told the group about their visit to the hospital, and Pat seemed to have achieved some further reconciliation to hospitalization.

"It isn't where I would like Bonnie to be," she said, "but there isn't any other place." Her yearning for a better solution was expressed in her wish to visit another state hospital of which she had heard, but Brad pointed out that the only difference would be geographic. His mind seemed quite made up, and it was evident that the long-postponed action was about to be taken. Pat had succeeded in bringing herself to discuss the placement plan with her oldest daughter, who had responded with interested questions. The younger children still had not been told.

The dilemma and the challenge which life had brought to this couple were different in a significant way from others we have been discussing. For the other parents mentioned in this book, the achievement of progress in their own life adjustment brought the concomitant reward of enabling them to meet the emotional needs of their handicapped child more fully. Through their own personal and individual growth, they could better provide a family setting which would facilitate the optimal development of the handicapped child within the structure of his limitations. Most of the parents who participated in my group had the satisfaction of seeing their own therapeutic progress reflected in gains of some kind shown by the handicapped child. Such satisfaction was not possible for Pat and Brad.

The cruelly painful reality which life had brought to them was the fact of their utter helplessness to improve Bonnie's level of functioning, regardless of what they did. It is always frustrating for man to come up against the absolute limits of his power. The history of mankind is replete with instances of man's attempts to prove himself more powerful than he really is. Those are chronicles of love of power for power's sake. But when the powerlessness is experienced in connection with a thwarted humanitarian goal, it has a special poignancy. And when the powerlessness is experienced in relationship with one's own child, whom one is powerless to help, the pain is very deep.

One element which must inevitably arise in connection with such pain is a sense of guilt about taking advantage of one's own capacity for personal fulfillment in the face of such tragic lack of capacity in another. As Brad clarified in the group, the choice which he and Pat had had to face was the choice between letting Bonnie go in order that her parents and brothers and sisters could better fulfill their own capacity for living, or keeping Bonnie and devoting their lives to her care, with the attendant sacrifice of normal family life and the right to the pursuit of personal fulfillment. While the other parents in my group could best help their child by helping themselves, these parents had to choose between the two goals. No one can tell parents in such a dilemma which choice to make. As I told these parents, my own feelings were in the direction of wishing that they would hospitalize the child in order to free themselves and their other children for the utilization of life's gifts, but only they could really make the decision.

In a sense, all people of humanitarian feeling face a similar dilemma on a less directly personal level. When I sit down to a bountiful and delicious meal, I have to put aside my concern for the child who is dying of starvation in some area remote from me. I can contribute my bit to a relief fund to send food to that starving child, but I am powerless to do anything about the fact that the food may rot, lying undelivered at a remote airstrip where it sits in the sun. The powerlessness I feel about this is on the same dimension as the powerlessness felt by these parents, but their pain is infinitely deeper and more personal. Their pain is acute and also pervasive, like a smoke which seeps under all doors and enters every room of their lives. The challenge they now face is to be able to utilize and enjoy the gifts of life despite the presence of its pain.

CHAPTER SEVEN

The Catalytic Impact of Tears

Working therapeutically with parents of handicapped children is essentially no different from the therapeutic work I would do with any parents who came to me for help with family problems. The extent to which I can be of help to anyone who comes to me is partially determined by the extent to which that person is able to drop his defensive guard and enter the inner realm of his own disturbed feelings. This is true regardless of the nature or source of the inner disturbance.

In order to understand this, you have to know something about how psychological defense systems are formed. Psychological defenses are unconscious ways of coping with the stresses and strains of life. We all form these defensive patterns in the process of growing up, and they become part of the structure of our developing personality. You may find it surprising to think of children as needing to form defenses against the stresses and strains of life because you may think of childhood as an ideal period of life, devoid of pressures and problems. But when you think about it again, you realize that, of course, that is not true. The stream of life is never a continuous unbroken flow of satisfaction and gratifications. This delightful flow is frequently broken by frustrations, irritations, disappointments, and demands which necessitate frequent readjustments of the inner needs to the outer realities. The ways in which the child unconsciously makes these readjustments determine the patterns of his developing personality and of his psychological defense systems.

Parents sometimes feel that they should be able to provide their children with such an ideal environment and such a problem-free life that the children will grow up perfectly adjusted and free of any inner problems. Such a goal cannot be achieved, because such perfection is not within the realm of human life. Even if it were possible for such perfection to be achieved, the outcome would boomerang into an even greater problem, for the child would grow up without ever shedding his unconscious belief that he is the center of the world. The infant and very young child have no realization that they are not the center of the world, but a healthy part of growing up is the dawning realization by the child that he is only one among many people, all of whose needs contribute to the stream of life.

So we come back to the point that the developing child must learn to adjust his needs to the realities of the world around him; and, in the process of doing this, he unconsciously builds into his personality psychological patterns of defense. Some of these defenses will be sufficiently flexible in nature that they can serve him all his life; but others, particularly those formed under greater stress, will be rigid and will later come to interfere with his possibilities for healthy living. When these defense patterns were formed, they were the best way the child could cope with whatever pressures were upon him. However, since they were formed under stress, they are characterized by a rigidity which perpetuates them when they are no longer needed or useful. When the child becomes an adult, these rigid defenses are still very much a part of him and tend to operate in situations which really do not require them. Because they are inappropriate, they stand in the way of healthier adjustment patterns which might otherwise develop. Because they are unconscious, the person has no awareness of them as a part of himself or as an interference with his living.

As adults, therefore, we have to find some way of breaking through this interfering system of defenses and of entering the realm of feeling and emotion which they are keeping out of our conscious awareness. As children, we could not be conscious enough to deal with all our feelings and emotions directly, but as adults we are much more capable of achieving such conscious awareness and we will grow and develop as persons by doing so.

It is my function as psychotherapist to help my adult patients gain conscious awareness of the operation of their defense systems so they can become more fully the masters of their own functioning, rather than remaining at the mercy of unknown forces within themselves. By gaining perspective on their defenses, they are also able to break through them to the inner realm of emotions that must be brought into the open and understood. All of this results in the evolvement of healthier patterns of functioning and the development of inner strength. When parents are thus able to grow, their children reap indirect benefits.

As you would expect, the people who come to me vary greatly in their readiness for this kind of therapeutic work. This was true of those who joined my group for parents of cerebral palsied children. As a therapist, I find it important to ascertain a person's degree of readiness for relinquishing some of his defenses. If a person clings tightly to his established defense system and shows no indication of conflict about it, it is often best to leave it alone and work with the patient at the level he chooses, even though this may mean that many important inner feelings are not brought to light. In a sense, this was true of Pat, for most of her deepest feelings about Bonnie's tragic impairment were never talked about in our group. It is possible that, had they been released into conscious awareness and expression, they would have been too painful and too strong to be worked through in the nine-month period she was in the group.

Harriet, who with her husband had joined the group at the same time as had Pat and Brad, was already experiencing a breakdown of her defense system when she came. In protecting herself from the severe insecurities and deprivations of her early years, she had formed an image of herself as a strong and independent person who did not give in to her emotions, who aggressively met life head on, and who resolutely carried any responsibilities life brought her. The difficulty with this defense system was that it left no room for awareness of her own emotional needs, her inner vulnerabilities, nor feelings of weakness or fear. As the mother of four children aged five and younger, one of whom was seriously cerebral palsied, she was constantly subjected to pressures and strains, and she had not developed adequate ways of living with her own emotional reactions. This would be difficult for anyone to do, but Harriet was handicapped by her repressive overcontrol of herself.

The inevitable result of this situation was that Harriet's defense system was breaking down without her volition or conscious awareness. This took the form of sudden and unexpected eruptions of her temper, and it was concern about this which brought her to my group. In the initial individual session, she was able to verbalize frankly that she did not "want to be here," but she knew she needed to come. She was also able to admit her fear of entering the group without the supporting presence of her husband, Randy, who was therefore also going to attend. In making these admissions, she was already lowering her defensive shield in a healthy way. We have to befriend our weaker sides in order to become truly strong.

Harriet and Randy presented a somewhat confusing picture of the condition of their three-year-old son Ernie. As a young infant, he had undergone heart surgery, and his cerebral palsy had subsequently come to light gradually in the usual torturous way. Through paralysis and spasticity, the child was limited in the use of his left side and unable to walk. About this, Harriet made the comment that visitors to their home are mystified about who could need the wheelchair, and are amazed when told it belongs to Ernie. Harriet also said that, although Ernie is mentally retarded, people "simply can't believe it because he is so bright." Whereas some parents present the problem of trying to hide behind their child's handicap, these parents continued talking with the apparent objective of convincing me that there was really nothing wrong with Ernie. Anticipating their future need for help in coming to a realistic acceptance of Ernie's handicap, I commented simply that it is difficult to ascertain the mental status of a three-year-old child with a possible speech defect.

Returning to the subject of her own inner tensions, Harriet confided an incident which had occurred late in her pregnancy with Ernie. She had come very close to violent attack upon her oldest son and had been terrified by her own behavior. Her attempts to utilize psychiatric help at that time had come to nothing, and she now felt strongly motivated to join this group. Much of her concern lay with her oldest son Warren, whom she described as "volatile and trigger-tempered like his mother." She remarked that she has relaxed more with each successive child, but that she felt it was a wonder that Warren had survived.

In the group sessions, Harriet seemed to have lost contact with her own motivation for working on her problems. In the presence of the other parents, her defenses came up and she communicated in a way that seemed to be designed to convey an image of herself as someone who had all the answers. Her very clever wit introduced an element of humor into the group, but this had the effect of separating people from their own emotions, thus retarding the therapeutic work. When other parents succeeded in bringing up their problems, Harriet glibly provided solutions by citing material about other people she knew or magazine articles she had read.

This therapeutic impasse was broken by one of the mothers, Rita, who had attended the group the previous year. She had been waiting all summer to bring up a dream which she had had just after the final session the previous spring. This dream involved Rita's childhood relationship with her parents, and she released a good deal of emotion as the group worked with her on the problem. This deepened the level of communication within the group, and subsequent sessions were more productive therapeutically.

Harriet's difficulty in opening up before the group stemmed from her inability to accept her negative feelings toward her children. All parent-child relationships have some ambivalence or mixture of positive and negative feelings. Harriet's lack of flexibility about this drove her negative feelings underground, and they tended to erupt unpredictably, under the pressure of her maternal responsibilities. She wanted to be rid of this explosive symptom, but was unconsciously resistant to the necessary step of facing her negative feelings.

One of the values of group therapy is that a person who is highly defended in a particular area may be exposed to the emotional impact of someone who is more open in a similar area. As we saw in Chapter Five, Jean was such a person. Having found during the first year of the group that it provided her with a much-needed opportunity for cathartic release of emotions, Jean was usually tearful and unguarded in her explorations of her own maternal experiences. This disturbed Harriet because it stimulated her own unconscious need for cathartic release.

In one session, Jean had been discussing some of the pressures of family life with Brad, whom you met in Chapter Six. It was at this time that Brad went more fully into the seriousness of the condition of his little defective daughter Bonnie, and he then confided to the group for the first time that the strain had become so great that he and Pat had started to consider permanent hospitalization for Bonnie. At this point, Harriet broke in and directed a query to Jean.

"Excuse me," she said, "but have you ever considered boarding Jenny out?"

"No," said Jean firmly, and Harriet persisted, "But under the circumstances, the way you're feeling almost constantly, you're still not considering it?"

"No," Jean replied firmly again. Harriet's lack of emotional flexibility was revealed here in her inability to understand that Jean could struggle with her emotional limitations as her own problem without needing to act them out by getting rid of the child. Harriet was also failing to note here the differential in severity of handicap between Bonnie and Jean's daughter, Jenny.

Whereas Bonnie was so severely impaired both mentally and physically that no amount of parental care and sacrifice could really help her to develop, Jenny's potential for physical improvement was fairly good and her intelligence high. I did not enter the discussion with an explanation of these facts because I saw here the beginning of a therapeutic unfolding. If I had explained the matter to Harriet, she would have understood the explanation on an intellectual level, but her defense system and her suppressed feelings would have remained untouched. As a therapist, I must time my remarks so that they do not interfere with the unfolding of the person's inner feelings.

After a period of silence, Brad began talking about the difficulty he and Pat had in trying to get a weekend off, or even an evening. Because a child's handicap complicates the baby-sitting problem, all the group members were involved and joined in the discussion. I reflected their feeling that having a handicapped child sometimes made them feel trapped, whereupon Harriet protested that they *shouldn't* feel that way. Rita said that it's only natural to have such feelings; Harriet then admitted that she *does* feel a wish not to have more children. Then, as if stunned by her own admission, she exclaimed, "It's horrible of me to say that!"

As she sat there, overwhelmed by guilt feelings and condemning herself for what she had said, I tried to help her to see that the problem was her self-condemning attitude itself. She defensively denied any guilt feeling, insisting, "Objectively it is horrible for me to sit here and say that I don't want any more children as long as I live!" I, in turn, insisted that this is not an objective fact but rather a subjective evaluation involving guilt feelings, and that I would like her to recognize it as such, the recognition being an essential first step toward letting go of the guilt feeling. Somewhat subdued, she accepted this and then went on to confide to the group some of the upset feelings that often boil up in her and are then taken out on her children in angry physical attacks on them. By then, the two-hour session had come to a close, but the therapeutic process had started working for Harriet.

In the following session, Harriet participated without her usual need to distract from the substance of the communication. At a propitious moment, she reintroduced her problem of loss of emotional control, having brought the subject up in the previous week's session. She did so by relating an incident that had occurred involving her oldest son Warren, not yet five. They had been entering a school yard that had iron gates, when he said, "Don't slam it on me!"

"Now whatever made you think that I would slam a big old heavy gate on your head?" she had asked.

"Then why do you beat up on me?" he replied in turn. The child's penetrating query gave her pause and strengthened her emerging motivation to bring the problem to the group. She confessed quite openly that when her temper boils she unleashes a truly vicious attack upon Warren. With encouragement from the group, Harriet told about mistreatment she had received as a child. Then, expressing her sense of desperation about her own temper, she exclaimed, "That's why I'm here!" She seemed to be telling us, "You should give me a prescription for self-control."

I asked Harriet if she ever has advance awareness of the tensions building up in her, and she replied by describing how her temper would suddenly boil over: "Boom! Like that!" It was clear that the demands of the four children exerted a tremendous pressure on her, and that she functioned better in the evening hours, when Randy was at home to relieve her. Sometimes, when she was subjected to pressure from the children in the presence of other people, she would burst into tears and go off somewhere to cry. "This," she asserted, "is ridiculous!"

I explained that tears are nature's way of providing release, and that this is much better than exploding at the children.

"Oh, yes," she replied. "I guess so. I really don't know." It was hard for Harriet to accept the natural release of tears because of her need to view herself as strong. Although it was difficult, at the time, to evaluate how much benefit Harriet received through this communication, it was encouraging that a few sessions later she reported that her little boy, Warren, had come to her with a request to be kissed. As this was a most unusual event in their relationship, it seemed that therapeutic benefit might be carrying over into her home.

It is characteristic of the therapeutic process that periods of progress are usually followed by periods of retrenchment. This seemed true of Harriet in several subsequent sessions, as she again retreated from her problem and tried to present an idealized image of her maternal functioning. At home, in her efforts to curb the acting-out of her negative feelings toward her children, she was again suppressing them from her awareness. Once the process of self-confrontation has started, however, it has an inner momentum of its own. Harriet's deeply buried feelings of aloneness, helplessness, and despair had begun crying for expression. In conflict with these feelings were Harriet's suppressive and repressive defenses, and this conflict within her was again being stirred up and aroused by Jean's cathartic release of feelings within the group. Since the conflict in Harriet was unconscious, her defensive reaction took the form of a need to bring Jean's feelings under control in the suppressive way that she handled her own upsets.

One evening, several group members were late, and only Harriet and Rita were present at the outset. Harriet, who was at this time in retreat from facing her own difficulties as a mother, began expressing her conflict unconsciously by focusing on Jean's relationship to Jenny. Again asserting her opinion that Jean should consider placing Jenny in a boarding home, Harriet stated, "This is the way I see Jean—that she loves the child, but the child's getting to be too much for her, and she's beating her head against the wall. She cries every night she comes here, without fail!"

The therapeutic challenge here was to help Harriet reach beyond her defensive preoccupation with Jean to her own conflicting maternal feelings. In trying to bring Harriet back to an awareness of her own inner conflict, I pointed out that there is strength in the ability to know one's own negative feelings and to give them expression in nonharmful ways. When I commented that Harriet kept a tight rein on herself because of her wish to be a good parent, Harriet laughed, asking, "Can you see that halo?"

At this point, several other group members entered the room, and the level of communication shifted. At an appropriate time, I picked up the threads of the interrupted conversation by saying, "So, to go on—" and Harriet came in quickly with a question about her halo. I reiterated my view that she is so concerned with presenting the image of a good mother that she keeps a tight rein on any expression of bad feelings within the group and that she would probably have less inner tensions if she could let her bad feelings show and let all her feelings flow more freely, as Jean does. Harriet protested that she does let her feelings out too freely—toward her children.

"But I mean here," I said, "with us."

"Well, that's just it," Harriet conceded. "Maybe I'm not letting them out in the right place."

Harriet then talked of her "need for a halo," saying she might benefit from having that need broken up now, although she had had to erect it in defense against the expectation she had lived with as a child that she would grow up to be no good. Jean told Harriet that, on the way home the previous week, she had told her husband, Paul, that Harriet seemed so sure that she knew "what the right way is," whereas Jean herself had to search for the right way.

"If you feel that way," Harriet stated authoritatively, "life is going to be hell! You've got to make some way to go." As she continued elaborating her position to Jean, she kept her gaze directed toward me. I drew her attention to this, adding that most of the participants, except Brad, were looking at me, even though obviously talking to someone else.

Brad then spoke to Jean about how difficult decisions seemed to be for her, and Jean answered by referring to some of the problems she had been working on. Harriet stated in punctuated tones, "But Jean, you're *always* stirred up!" As Harriet continued emphasizing her point, her own feelings began to slip out: "*I* can't go on stirred up! I had too much as a child! I couldn't possibly go through life as you do."

Again I asked her, "Why can't you address that to Jean?"

"I can't stand—" Harriet broke off in an outburst of tears.

"—to see her cry," I finished for her, and Harriet said, "Yes." After a moment she added, "This is one reason why I didn't think I was going to like this group."

"All this emotion flying around," I again finished for her, and again she said, "Yes."

"You've been able to hide your own emotions like I have," Brad told Harriet. "Deep inside to a degree. To see it come out in the open from somebody else disturbs us—no, it doesn't disturb me."

"Well, it disturbs me!" Harriet cried with unusual frankness. "And I'm sitting here and keeping a tight rein on myself!"

"You're keyed up more than I am," said Brad.

"Oh, Lord," moaned Harriet, going on to tell of an incident in which a doctor had described her as "extremely nervous." Accepting the Kleenex box, she exclaimed, "I get it from everybody! How does . . . everybody see this in me! And yet, I try to feel so calm inside, you know, and I'm not. I'm really not!" With desperation in her voice, she talked of how she had lived in an emotionally charged atmosphere from babyhood up, and of how she had been left with the feeling of not wanting to get attached to anything.

"I just had so much of it as a child that I can't hardly stand emotion," she concluded.

"And yet it's within you and needs to come out or it wouldn't be such a problem," I told her.

Turning the focus back to Jean, Harriet protested, "But with each and every meeting, Jean has broken down!" Facing Jean directly for the first time, she said, "I get the feeling that you love Jenny, but you don't know what to do with Jenny. You wish you did know what to do with Jenny, and you wish that the whole thing could be taken out of your hands. . . . As Brad says, you're too upset by this child that's six years old! You've had this child six years, and still you react this way—"

Her empathetic feeling for Jenny clearly visible, Jean sobbed, "I can't *stand* it when some kid comes in to play and can't understand a word that she says. This kills me! You wouldn't know it if you were there, because I'm cheery and bright and I'm there to help. But it's gnawing at me." Harriet insisted that the problem was that Jenny was getting older, and Brad presented detailed advice about how to handle the communication problem. Jean cited several incidents, illustrating that she did most of the things Brad was advising.

After a period of silence, Harriet said thoughtfully, "I don't know. You've given me something to think about—the halo bit. Maybe I just put the halo on when I go outside the home."

Telling Harriet that she does have a good opportunity here to let down her halo, I went on, "While there certainly is something to be concerned about in Jean's tears and her upset feelings, there is another side to it too. That is that I think Jean knows that *here* she can cry, and that all the feelings that she doesn't take out in destructive ways during the week can be sort of stored up and released here for catharsis. And I suspect that, really, in the home, Jean does pretty well, and I suspect that most of the time there's a pretty happy, free-and-easy atmosphere with a lot of flexibility, and that Jenny feels her mother's support a great deal. Is this true, that you kind of store it up and release it here?"

"Yes," said Jean, "I do that."

"Because you know this is a place where you can—"

"I always feel kind of relieved after I've been here," Jean added.

"And you feel better, and then go back and tackle the problem a little better as a result of it. And, really, I wish there could be more of this." I told Harriet that her tensions may diminish when she becomes able to relinquish her need to keep proving things about herself and to allow herself the benefit of releasing her bad thoughts and feelings here.

"I think one reason Jean's tears are so distressing is because they bring up one's own need to cry," I told the group.

"It could very well be," agreed Harriet.

"And it might be that you could also benefit from letting your tears come up."

"Probably," Harriet agreed again. "If the day should come, I might flood the room."

This session was the turning-point for Harriet. This is not to imply that an overnight transformation occurred. Psychotherapy is always a slow and difficult process, with each two or three steps forward being followed by at least one step back. As Harriet became less defensive and began to reveal her own inner needs for sympathy and support, she was amazed to learn that the other members of the group had perceived her as "hardheaded and hardhearted." Rita said that she had thought that Harriet "didn't know how to cry," and Paul told Harriet that she usually seemed to be "so set on one path that you have cloudy thinking."

"Maybe I'm wrong in saying this," ventured Rita, "but I think the first thing you're going to have to get over is this shield you have wrapped around you." Harriet's fear of being seen as feeling sorry for herself came out, and her husband Randy joined with the group in reassuring Harriet that a person feeling sorry for himself is just reacting naturally.

The emotional storm which had long been brewing within Harriet broke during the last session before Christmas vacation and brought some of the relief which usually follows the precipitation of moisture. In this and later sessions, Harriet poured out much about the traumas life had brought her, during both childhood and adult years. For the first time, she went into the heartbreak of her infant son's heart surgery and the subsequent discovery of his cerebral palsy. This was eventually followed by an admission of her desperate need for time by herself, and then by admission of her feelings of wanting to be away from her children.

The fact that she received sympathetic support from the group, rather than the expected condemnation, further freed Harriet to disclose a problem which she had not felt able to share. This was the serious problem of Ernie's head-banging.

"It's unbelievable!" she asserted. "Ernie's crib is . . . it's a wonder it's not battered to pieces. We've padded it, we've put foam rubber this thick on it, which he's eaten and torn to shreds. We've padded it with quilts, we've padded it with blankets, we have anchored them under his mattress. . . . He rips them off, he pulls the blanket down, and crash-bang! Crash-bang! Crash-bang! Crash-bang! He's got a bald spot—a permanent bald spot—on the top of his head, and a lump to go with it! And this is . . . his crib is chewed to pieces. He eats anything—wood—anything!"

Having once disclosed this problem, Harriet seemed almost to need to dramatize it. It was indeed serious, for Ernie had been manifesting this head-banging behavior almost since infancy, and his two older brothers also manifested it, although to a lesser extent. The group discussed it as a possible reflection of Harriet's tension. I suggested their getting a rocking chair for the purpose of soothing Ernie at bedtime. Randy seemed to accept this suggestion; but, when I inquired about it in a later session, Harriet's opposition to the idea came into the open. She said that by Ernie's bedtime, both she and Randy were only too ready to get him into bed, and she feared there would be "danger of developing a bad habit." Harriet and Randy did go for consultation with a psychiatrist, who prescribed a tranquilizer for the child. However, in a later session, Harriet reported, "This will kill you. The tranquilizers they use for psychiatric patients, they gave Ernie—prescribed them for him. Ha! They're not doing a thing! He was banging his head this week three times worse than he's ever banged it before."

During this period, Harriet was under tension in connection with interviews preliminary to an evaluation of Ernie by the child development clinic. The group members continued to be supportive of her and involved in the problem of Ernie's head-banging. Rita suggested a sponge rubber helmet for the child and helped Harriet to make one. Randy and Harriet returned to the psychiatrist for further consultation, and were told to eliminate the child's daytime use of the tranquilizer and to double his nocturnal dosage. Gradually, the head-banging began to diminish.

As Ernie's Clinic Day approached, Harriet was able to confide her fear that Ernie might be taken from her. She now welcomed the supportive interest of the group in her feelings; and, attending despite a severe cold, she explained that she would hate to miss a session. She felt that she had gained not only in the understanding of her own problems but also in the realization that others have problems too. She was applying her new-found capacity for insight to problems in her functioning as a mother, and she voiced her discovery that her past was not "dead and buried" but had been helping to shape her current perceptions, sometimes in damaging ways. In the session immediately preceding Ernie's Clinic Day, she had many questions, reflecting primarily her need for reassurance, which I tried to provide.

Following Ernie's Clinic Day, the group was interested in learning the outcome of the evaluation, and Harriet told them, "We got the worst kind of news. It hit me pretty hard; and, when I had to tell Randy, it hit him pretty hard, too. Ernie is severely mentally retarded and, according to them, he'll never be able to make a living. And he will always need custodial care." As Ernie's mental retardation had been diagnosed as moderate rather than severe, Harriet's description of the clinic findings was a bit exaggerated, but it clearly revealed the emotional impact on her of this confirmation of a reality which had been hard for her to face. Ernie's mental age had been established at about fifteen months; and, although Harriet held on to certain reservations, she was already doing quite well in achieving acceptance of the findings.

Jean was interested in Harriet's appraisal of the clinic, and Harriet's response was surprisingly positive in view of her customary fear and resentment of authority structures. She had been particularly relieved that Ernie was thought to be doing satisfactorily at home and that there was no indication that he should not remain there. The only context in which his care outside of the home had been discussed was that of Harriet's expressed concern about what would happen to Ernie in case of loss of his parents. In this connection, Harriet had been advised to contact the Mental Retardation Unit and get Ernie on file there in case of any future need.

Having shared this much with the group, Harriet began to disclose a little of her subjective feelings toward the clinic and toward the time she had spent with me following the clinic visit and by telephone the next day. Of the problem of assimilating the reality of Ernie's mental limitations, she said, "I was aware and yet I was unaware."

Randy had remained completely silent, and I said that he must have many feelings, too. He replied that he still couldn't help believing that Ernie might have undiscovered possibilities, but that he recognized that this probability is slight. If the doctors were right, then he knew he must accept it, even though it is "a painful dose of medicine." He went on to speak of Ernie's needing to be cared for "as a baby" even though full grown. I explained that at maturity Ernie would not have the mind of a baby but of a young child. Randy then proceeded to clarify, in his own mind, Ernie's condition through reference to various limited persons he had observed over his life time. I worked with him in using this method of understanding. Randy felt particularly upset by the thought that Ernie would need custodial care, and I said that the necessity for this in the future would be a function not only of Ernie's condition but also of "the overall situation in terms of other people who care enough about him to make up the balance." I referred also to the comment that had been made at the clinic that community resources are gradually improving. Harriet responded to this by reemphasizing that she had no thought at that time of placing Ernie outside of the home and that she did not know whether she would be able to do this if it should become necessary at some future time. She recalled at this point the clinic's recommendation that the family situation be reevaluated every six months. "I'm beginning long-range planning in my mind now," she said.

After a silence, Harriet opened up to the group the intense resentment she had felt against me and against the clinic doctors on the Friday night following the conference. She cried as she said, "Here I was blissfully ignorant of the whole situation—aware and yet unaware. And I felt that Dr. Heisler had forced me into the situation, and I asked Randy, 'Why couldn't they let me be?'" Then she added, "I don't resent you today," and I told her that it was all right for her to have those resentful feelings. She said that she now realized that these things have to be faced. She also knew that I had not forced her but that I had perceived her readiness to face them better than she was able to know.

In the remaining sessions of the group, Harriet's comments about her handicapped son revealed a much more realistic appraisal and acceptance of his current capabilities and limitations. Particularly pleasing to everyone was the news that Ernie's head-banging had completely stopped. With the other children, also, Harriet seemed better able to cope with problems although her inner tensions were far from resolved.

Through explorations of her own childhood, she was beginning to see connections between certain frustrations which she had been unwittingly imposing upon her children and experiences of sadistic treatment to which she had been subjected as a child. Expressing interest in evaluating her own therapeutic progress, she said that in some ways she felt worse, for therapy "damages what you've already thought of yourself." With a laugh, she added, "I'm examining myself more and liking it less!"

In the final session Harriet asked me, "Do you think I've improved at all?" and I replied that I did indeed.

"I think, Harriet, you've mellowed, or else I've come to know you better," said Jean. "I have the feeling about you of more softness."

"Well, something has occurred," Harriet agreed. "I got the most left-handed compliment the other day. This salesgirl at the store came out with it. She said, 'What's happened to you? You look so much better! You used to look—', and then she realized what she was saying, you know, and she said, 'I mean—you look more rested.' " After a pause, Harriet added, "I guess it's a general easing of a lot of things."

Harriet herself realized that this brief therapeutic journey was merely a beginning of the self-exploratory task that would be necessary for deeper and more long-term gains both in her family relationships and in her inner development. Nevertheless, the gains that she had made in this brief time were very real and very important for the welfare of her children.

CHAPTER EIGHT

Your Child Has Inner Resources

A book on parental adjustment to a child's handicap is necessarily a book on parent-child relationships because the parent's adjustment to the handicap of the child is an aspect of the total relationship between that parent and child. The principles of constructive parental functioning are the same for both handicapped and non-handicapped children, but the application of these principles always varies according to the specific factors involved, and the existence of the handicap does introduce special considerations.

The most controversial question today in the area of parent-child relationships is the question of authoritarianism versus permissiveness in parental discipline. Because the principle involved in this question has a very important special significance in the case of the physically handicapped child, it is necessary to go into it here. The principle of which I speak has to do with the development of the child's potential for self-direction. Except for the child's basic security-need, which is fulfilled through parental love, there is no psychological need more important to the child's later maturity and stability than the development of his potential capacity for self-direction. This fact has not been understood by thousands of parents who have tried to apply the psychologically popular concept of permissiveness and have thereby released their children to a state of freedom from discipline without accompanying nurturance of the child's inner resources for responsible and productive functioning.

The original meaning of the concept of parental permissiveness was that the parent would permit the child freedom to find his own individual ways of self-expression and problem-solving. The constructively permissive parent would continue to be involved and related with the child while permitting him this freedom. Too many parents have not understood that the goal of permissiveness was to support the development of the child's own inner resources. Confused about the meaning of the concept, they have misapplied it. They have used the concept of permissiveness as an excuse and justification for withdrawing from parental responsibility. Saying to themselves, "I am told by psychologists that I should not force my will upon my child but should let him have his own way," they have failed to set limits when the child needed limits to curb his impulsiveness or his unrealistic sense of his own power.

Careful thought is required of a parent in order to evaluate when a child needs free rein and when he needs to be curbed, and decisiveness is required of a parent in order to carry out the evaluation. Many parents find it hard to be decisive and to say "No" to a child. Many parents cannot give up an overly authoritarian or harshly disciplinarian approach without going to the opposite extreme and abandoning their sense of parental responsibility. The results of this are being seen today in the sense of confusion and disorientation that besets much of youth, and the opponents of permissiveness are saying "I told you so." It would be unfortunate for the concept of permissiveness to fall into disrepute, because it has great value if applied with an understanding of its goal of facilitating development of the capacity for self-direction.

This goal has special significance and importance for the physically handicapped child. It is really tragic when a physically dependent person carries the added handicap of emotional dependence on external direction and control. Such psychological reinforcement of a physical limitation is particularly destructive to the spirit of the handicapped person. On the other hand, the physically handicapped person who is psychologically independent and self-directing may be characterized by great strength of spirit. This inner spirit may be developed in the process of overcoming the many obstacles to fulfillment that inevitably lie in the path of the handicapped person, but this will happen only if the person is motivated from within toward the achievement of his own goals.

The ability to form one's own goals and to work toward them does not develop overnight, and it does not develop easily in adult life if no opportunity has been allowed for its gradual development while growing up. One cannot remain an obedient child without self-direction for eighteen or twenty-one years and then transform suddenly into a responsible adult. On the other hand, the first two decades of life are a period of natural emotional dependence on the parents, who have the responsibility for gratifying the youngster's security needs. Emotional security is given to the child through parental love, understanding, interest and involvement, empathy, and, also, through the setting of limits when the youngster's expanding energies and activities exceed the boundaries of what is safe for him. Within such a security-structure provided by the parents, the child needs freedom to make choices of his own and to develop his own values, standards, and goals.

This is as true for the physically handicapped child as for the nonhandicapped. The challenge to parents is complicated in the case of the handicapped child whose physical dependence may cause the parents to lose sight of his capacity for the development of self-direction. Over the passing years of his childhood, his mobility may remain at the level of a much younger child, and his parents may continue to treat him as if he really were that young. The common parental tendency to overdirect and overcontrol their children may be more pronounced toward the handicapped child, whose physical dependence makes it easier for his parents to control him. This can have particularly tragic consequences since this child's ability to function is already limited and overcontrolled by his physical handicap. It is imperative for his psychological development that he be given freedom to make his own choices to the extent that is possible within the limiting framework of his handicap.

You may agree with me but still feel that you do not know *how* to do this. The ways in which you can grant freedom of choice to your handicapped child will change and expand over the years of his childhood. This is, of course, true for all children. Many parents do not realize the extent to which even very young children are capable of a natural, unconscious self-direction which is motivated toward their own healthy development. This may be observed, for example, in the area of feeding. Infants tend to regulate their own quantity of food intake through their physiological and psychological states of hunger and satiety. Young children also have a natural ability to do this, but anxious parents may create feeding problems by insisting that the child eat more than he wants or by insisting that he eat some food which is at that moment distasteful to him. If this parental pattern of force-feeding becomes pronounced, the child will develop an inner resistance to being controlled and a real feeding problem will develop. Parents who are overly anxious about their child's nourishment and who exert too much control over his eating often wonder why their child does not have the healthy appetite of the child down the street. Chances are that the child with the healthy appetite has been permitted more freedom of choice about what and how much he eats.

The development of a battle of wills over feeding may be particularly damaging to the physically handicapped child because of the restriction of his physical activity. The normally active child's rebellious refusal to eat may be counteracted by the stimulation to his appetite from a period of play out-of-doors. The physically handicapped child, on the other hand, has less opportunity of this kind to break out of the rut of inner resistance to being forced to eat, so he may develop a real aversion to food.

This has regrettable consequences for his physical health, as well as for his psychological health. I often hear a mother saying that it is because of her concern over her child's physical health that she tries to force him to eat. It is, of course, true that there may be special circumstances in which the child's doctor has prescribed a certain food or medicine which the child will not take unless the parent insists. In this case, the wise mother will be decisive and firm in her insistence. However, her insistence in such special circumstances will be more effective if the overall pattern of her relationship with her child is one in which she permits him latitude of choice in his eating.

It may be reassuring to parents to know of one psychological research study in which children under two years of age with known nutritional deficiencies were offered a wide assortment of foods and were permitted to make their own choices. To a statistically significant extent, the foods voluntarily chosen by these young children were the foods which were most appropriate for the treatment of their own particular type of deficiency. I mention this study to point out that the human organism has its own inherent, unconscious wisdom. Your child has within him a potential for healthy self-direction which will unfold like the growth and blossoming of a plant if this potential is nurtured and not blocked or damaged.

Of course, the nurturing of your child's potential is important. Even the hardiest of plants will not survive, grow, and unfold without the necessary environmental conditions. In providing this nurturance, however, you must remember that you are nurturing a potential that is already there within your child and your responsibility is only to help it unfold. So many times mothers have asked me, "How can I make my child *do* this?" or "How can I make my child *be* that?" The truth is that you really cannot *make* your child do or be anything. You can only *help* him to become who he already potentially is. That is, you can help him to *actualize the potential* that is already within him. I hope that by knowing this you will feel relieved of the burden carried by parents who think they have to shape and mold their child's personality.

On the other hand, parents can do harm by blocking the unfolding of the child's potential. The two most common ways in which parents of handicapped children block their child's development are through pushing and overprotecting. These are two opposite extremes of parental behavior which have a common underlying factor. Both pushing and overprotecting a child reflect the parents' lack of faith in the child's own inner resources. Both of these approaches make it more difficult for the child to discover and develop his own resources. If you are overly protective, you are holding your child back, interfering with his initiative and taking away his courage. On the other hand, if you push him, you are also interfering with his initiative by taking away *his* opportunity to find his own motivation at his own level of readiness. In fact, when you push a child, you *decrease* his motivation for doing the thing you want him to do, because you are stimulating resistance to your own domination. The child's instinctual need for the right to self-direction makes it more important to him to withstand your domination than to do the thing in question.

Parents of physically handicapped children experience this dilemma particularly with regard to their child's physical development. In Chapters One and Two, we have already looked at the case of Mark, whose resistance to taking his exercises developed in opposition to pushing by his parents. Both these well-meaning parents were genuinely concerned about their son's welfare and believed that was their sole motivation for pushing him. However, as Lois worked on her own emotional problems in the therapy group, her tendency to push Mark diminished and gradually disappeared. This change reflected the fact that, unconsciously, her pushing of her son had stemmed from her own inner tensions. She was, in fact, pushing herself to be different from what she naturally was. As she came to realize and accept within herself feelings which she had not previously faced, her pattern of pushing Mark to exercise dropped away; he responded by finding his own motivation for exercising. The message from this, which I have tried to emphasize throughout this book, is that in any problem with your children you would do well to look first to your own emotional state and try to get a perspective on your own functioning in the problem situation. As your own unconscious contributants to the problem drop by the wayside, you are freer to look at the child's difficulties objectively and to consider the ways in which you can truly be of help to him.

One mother talked with me about her four-year-old daughter, whose walking had been retarded by her physical impairment. The child had improved sufficiently that her ability to walk was now emerging, but, still, walking was so difficult that the child preferred to crawl. The child had initially responded with pleasure to her new-found ability; but, as the mother tried to encourage her to walk, she seemed to become less motivated to do so. The mother's question to me was, "How can I motivate my little girl to want to walk when walking requires so much effort that she resists it?"

Such a challenge requires of the mother both ingenuity and the flexibility to sense and work with the child's changing moods. A person's level of motivation for any activity varies from hour to hour and even from moment to moment. If this mother's relationship with her little girl is close and sensitive, she will be able to tune in on the child's emotional state and catch the right moment for offering her hand or arm to the child for a practice session in walking. If the child gives a positive response to the offer, it is right to go ahead. If the child is hesitant, a bit of encouragement might be given, but, if the child is resistant, the offer should be dropped. Compelling the child to try will only add to the tension or fear that may already be there.

In general, it is wise to provide the child with situations which will elicit his own motivation. The mother of the four-year-old girl devised ways of placing her daughter's play toys out of her reach from a crawling position. She would help the child to her feet in a different part of the room so that the child could get her toys only by walking to them. When the little girl plopped herself down on the floor and cried for her toys, the mother found it difficult not to give in and get them for her. However, by abstaining from such overprotective behavior, she left her little daughter free to work through her own dependent feelings and find her own motivation for getting her own toys. And this the child did.

It is often a fine line that the parent must discriminate in order to avoid pushing, on the one hand, or overprotecting, on the other. The key to seeing this fine line is to remember that the child has his own motivational resources. For the human being, walking is the primary means of implementing the desire for locomotion, and the desire for locomotion is in turn motivated by other desires. The little girl's wish for her toys was such a motivating desire. If you try to gratify every conscious wish of your handicapped child immediately, you rob him of his own motivation for independent activity. He is capable of experiencing the frustration of trying and failing and trying again. The physically handicapped child who is not overprotected soon learns that in the realm of physical functioning, life requires more effort from him than from others. He is capable of accepting this requirement from life. What he needs from you is respect for his developing capabilities, combined with the security of knowing that you will lovingly provide that help which he really cannot do without.

One mother of a handicapped child once remarked to me that she found herself constantly faced with the necessity of evaluating her child's capabilities and of making decisions about her own functioning in relation to him. This is one of the realities of living constructively with physical handicap: namely, that it requires conscious evaluation and decision-making in situations where lack of physical handicap permits more spontaneous and even instinctual functioning. As the parent of a physically handicapped child, you carry the responsibility for achieving realistic expectations for your child's ability to function. This is necessary in order for you to know when your help is actually required and when that help would be overprotective. In this you have the help of your child's orthopedist, physical therapist, and others. However, their help only gives you a framework of knowledge within which you still must make moment-to-moment evaluations in the specific situations that arise over the course of the day. The problem is, of course, complicated by the fact that your child's capabilities do not stay at one level. In addition to the natural fluctuations in the child's level of motivation, there are changes in his actual level of physical capability as he makes progress through his physical therapy. It is important that you become able to observe and listen quietly, for this is your best source of knowledge and understanding of your child's changing physical capabilities. If the psychological and emotional climate that you provide is conducive to healthy functioning in your child, he will naturally make use of his physical gains and you will be able to see his progress.

It is not possible to overemphasize the importance to the handicapped child of opportunities for pleasurable activities. Because his handicap excludes him from many natural sources of childhood fun, it is easy for him to feel left out of life. Your ingenuity may again be tapped in finding ways to make fun available to him, and fun with other children is of particular importance. As the mother of a handicapped child, you will probably find yourself in the position of having other children in your home more often than would be the case if your child had normal mobility. A yard full of play equipment that can be enjoyed by normally active children, in addition to sand boxes and special equipment for the handicapped child, will enhance the setting in which other neighborhood children can get acquainted with your child and learn to understand and accept his limitations without depreciating him.

Sometimes other children need time and help in coming to an acceptance of the handicapped child. If you are able to be objective in your reaction to this, it will be easier for your handicapped child to be objective also. I have known of handicapped children whose objectivity about such things exceeded that of their parents. A poignantly impressive illustration of this came from one of the fathers in my therapy group. His ten-year-old cerebral palsied son, Ken, attended a special school where the other children also had handicaps of various kinds. However, one afternoon he was waiting for his mother on the playground of the regular school where she taught. She had gone into the school office for a few minutes; when she returned, he was being taunted by a group of strange boys. She wisely restrained her impulse to rush in protectively. When Ken joined her a little later, she asked him, "Why did you stay with those boys when they were treating you like that?" Ken replied simply, "I was giving them time to get used to me."

Within the simplicity of Ken's reply, there was profound natural wisdom. It is true of the human being that he needs time and often help in becoming comfortable with that which is different from him. This can be seen very clearly, for example, in primitive cultures, where members of one tribe will view members of another tribe with suspicion and enmity. It is true at every level of civilization that people tend to be attracted to that which is familiar and to have some discomfort with that which is strange or unknown. To the extent that an individual has achieved a broad objective perspective on himself in relation to life and other people, he will be less threatened by the strange and unfamiliar. Physical handicap may be seen as threatening not only because it is strange rather than familiar, but also because it brings home the reality of man's vulnerability. The child or adult encountering a visibly impaired person may unconsciously feel, "That could happen to me, too."

For the person with normal physical ability, feelings of discomfort or disturbance in the presence of an impaired person will diminish as the possibilities for adjustment to the handicap become apparent. This is true not only of adults, but also of children, who are capable of much flexibility in accommodating to the physical limitations of a peer if they like him and enjoy being with him. Of course, normally active children do not want interference with their free play, but they probably have some play activities in which the limited child can participate, and they will include him if they have had an opportunity to know and like him.

As a parent, you may feel a strong wish to protect your handicapped child from the hurts that will inevitably come to him in a group of nonhandicapped children. Not only is he subjected to the pain and frustration of seeing others do with enjoyment that which he cannot do, but he is also left open to the unguarded and frequently hurtful remarks of the other childen. It is an old truism that children can be very cruel, and the handicapped child in a group of normally active peers will probably be an occasional target of such cruelty. However, this kind of pain will be less harmful to him than the pain of being shut in or segregated from the general peer population of his world.

In refraining from overprotecting your child from this kind of hurt, however, you should not be cold, unsympathetic, or hard toward him. Your sympathetic understanding of his hurt and his tears when he brings them to you will be of major importance in enabling him to develop the inner strength needed to live with such hurts without giving up and withdrawing. Without your emotional support, he could come to feel that his handicap really makes him unacceptable; with your support, he can come to understand that when the other children reject him for being handicapped they are showing their own limitation and their need for help. One of the mothers in my therapy group remarked that, as parents of handicapped children, they have the responsibility for educating other people who have not had this problem in their lives. You can help your handicapped child to share this responsibility with you. His life experiences are of a kind which will inevitably sharpen his sensitivities, and sensitivity can be a precious gift when tempered by objectivity. Remember that, if you can be sensitive to your handicapped child's feelings and supportive of his inner development, he is capable of developing strength and objectivity.

Returning to the problem faced by the mother of the four-year-old girl who reverted to crawling after learning how to walk, this mother found that identification with other children became one of the motivating forces that contributed to the resolution of the problem. As the child was given an opportunity to play with normally active youngsters, her motivation for walking emerged out of desire to imitate them. Even play with younger children just learning to walk stimulated her desire to leave crawling behind and master the art of walking as they were doing.

The process of identification with others is one of the most basic and powerful forces in the development of the personality. The child's developing personality unconsciously absorbs and incorporates attributes of those around him, and the child's emerging sense of personal identity includes an identification with the world in which he lives. While any child's basic identifications occur within his family, they gradually extend to include the world outside his home also, and identification with peers is of great importance for his healthy development. For the physically handicapped child, it is essential to be given opportunities for participation and identification with nonhandicapped peers in order to facilitate his sense of belonging in the world outside his home.

Many benefits have come to the handicapped child through the development within school systems of segregated classes in which provisions can be made for working with his special limitations and needs. Without such classes, many handicapped children could not attend public school at all; and through such classes, handicapped children receive the help of specially trained and skilled personnel, who give the time and consideration necessary for finding ways in which the child can circumvent his handicap or compensate for it through substitute skills, in order to learn at the level of his mental capabilities and maximize his potential for productive functioning. The public schools deserve commendation for their fine work in providing these special services, and further such developments should be encouraged. As parents, you are to be commended for enabling your child to take advantage of these educational programs. He needs the very best assistance he can receive in equipping him for adult life.

However, as parents you must remember that education is not enough. Your handicapped child must also be given opportunities for identifying with the world of nonhandicapped people outside of his home, for it is in that world that he must make his way as an adult. The one disadvantage to your child of attending special classes for the handicapped is that he is deprived of the rich opportunity for relationships with nonhandicapped peers that he would have if he were able to attend nonsegregated classes. While he will develop valuable and meaningful friendships with other handicapped children in his special classes, he also needs to have friendships with nonhandicapped children, and you may have to find ways to make this possible. Friendships cannot develop if there is no contact.

Some handicapped children have access to such contacts through siblings (brothers and sisters) whose age is close to their own. However, it cannot be counted on that the siblings will want to include the handicapped child in any of their activities, and this cannot be required or forced by the parents. Such parental coercion would be sure to backfire on the handicapped child. In Chapter Four we met Jill, a young mother who felt deep conflict between her responsibility to her handicapped daughter, Doris, and the needs of Doris' two siblings. One of the ways in which help came to Doris was through a Girl Scout troop which admitted her even though not all of their activities were possible for her. Membership in the group had a tremendously rejuvenating effect on this youngster, who had been withdrawing into depression and apathy.

In such groups, acceptance by the other children is sometimes less a problem than acceptance by the adult in charge, who does not want responsibility for a handicapped child. Some such frightened adults refuse to admit the handicapped child, while others will admit him but then limit him unnecessarily. This was true of a Sunday School teacher, who admitted Jenny, whom you met in Chapter Five, to her class. One Sunday morning when Paul went to pick up Jenny at the time Sunday School ended, he found her sitting on her chair where she had sat for an hour-and-a-half watching the other children sprawled on the floor working with paper and crayons. She had tried to communicate to the teacher that she could lie on the floor and draw also, but the teacher had made no effort to understand what Jenny was saying and now used Jenny's speech defect as an excuse for not having known that

Jenny could do this. It was only with reluctance that she agreed to help Jenny to the floor and remove her brace the next time she introduced this kind of play activity, but in time and through Paul's help, she became more comfortable with the responsibility of a handicapped child, and the other children accepted Jenny as a regular member of their group.

Some of the parents in my therapy group found they could facilitate peer acceptance of their handicapped child through family outings to which they invited nonhandicapped neighborhood children. Since the limited mobility of the handicapped child makes it hard for him to reach out to the world, the parents may have to provide special bridges. Equipment designed according to the child's capabilities can also be of great help. Tricycles, for example, were found to be a possible mode of locomotion and activity for some of the children.

In your efforts to support your child's need for inclusion in the world outside the home, you must not fall into the opposite error of rejecting your child's dependency needs and his occasional retreats into the safety of the maternal fold. In the development of most children there is a natural alternation between the dependency needs, on the one hand, and the need to break away from the parents and participate in the world outside, on the other. This alternating rhythm, comparable to the ebb and flow of the ocean tides, can be seen most concretely in the play tendencies of a child of age five, six, or seven, who likes to be free to go in and out of the house at will. Playing with chums in the yard, he likes to be free to enter the house whenever he wishes, get what he wants, and return outside. Or, a child who has been threatened or hurt by an older or bigger child needs to be able to go home to mother for comfort or support without being discouraged from going back and facing the situation that frightened him. In fact, the mother's acceptance of his emotional dependence in such a situation is of the greatest help to him in becoming able to find his own inner courage for confronting the problem of his relationship with the other child. The child who is ostensibly reentering the house to get an object, such as food or another toy, is unconsciously reassuring himself that, by becoming more separate and independent of his mother, he is not jeopardizing his right to return to her. ·

The young child's natural rhythm of alternation between independent self-assertion and dependency needs may not be so concretely visible in the case of the handicapped child because he can not act it out so overtly. The very fact that his handicap limits his ability to live out this natural pattern of development renders the handicapped child even more vulnerable to unconscious conflict in the area of these two opposing inner tendencies. When any child is caught in unconscious conflict between these two inner personality forces, he is likely to show some symptoms of regression to an earlier age level. Such regressive symptoms are a signal to the mother that the child needs, on the one hand, support of his dependency needs and, on the other, support of his right to independent self-assertion.

One of the most frequent ways in which such an unconscious conflict in the child may be manifested is through enuresis (bedwetting). One mother talked with me about the ways in which she had been trying to cure the enuresis of her little physically handicapped daughter, who had developed this symptom as a result of starting school. Before reaching school age, the child had had very little contact with other children. Therefore, adjustment to school was for her a big step forward, with which she was confronted suddenly and without any gradual development of her inner resources for relating with other children or coping with strange situations outside her home. While the value of earlier opportunities for more gradual development had not been taken into consideration by the mother, she did now recognize that school was frightening to the child, and she was considering taking the child out of school. Since her various attempts to cure her little daughter's enuresis had failed, she was now beginning to feel that she had no recourse but to remove the child from school.

Without realizing it, this mother was using an approach that compounded the child's difficulty with both horns of the dilemma. By trying merely to cure the enuresis without accepting the needs manifested through the symptom, she was driving the dependency needs deeper. And, if she had removed the child from school, she would have cut off from the child an important source of stimulation for more independent functioning. The child's inability to respond positively to the challenge of school simply meant that it was too much for her to cope with all at once and without help. It did not mean that she was incapable of meeting the challenge at all.

The mother, who told me about the problem during the question-and-answer period following a public talk that I had given, focused her questioning on how she could cure the child's bed-wetting. Having only a brief opportunity for helping this mother, I told her pointedly, "You will never, never get anywhere trying to find ways to stop the bed-wetting. You have to change your focus entirely and think about the inner need in the child that is being manifested through the bed-wetting. As long as your focus is on stopping the bed-wetting, you *will* fail. When you become able to respond with maternal feeling to your little girl's baby-needs, you will give her a maternal nurturance which, in turn, will enable her to find her inner strength. Her need to be a baby *is* a retreat from the challenges of getting older; but, as you supply nurturance to her baby-needs, she will find more courage within herself for meeting those challenges. You must not protect her from that challenge. Do not take her out of school. Do not deprive her of the opportunity for finding her strength to function away from you. But when she is with you and needs to be held by you or cuddled, give this babying to her. When she goes to bed at night, sing to her or talk to her softly. But, in the morning, leave her at the school without indecision and don't look back. As she finds her inner resources and makes her adjustment to the school situation, her need for babying will recede, and she will gain more emotional independence."

A few months after this brief encounter, I received a telephone call from the mother, who wanted me to know that the change in her approach to the problem had produced the desired results and that her little girl was beginning to make a good school adjustment without needing so much special attention at home any more. The enuretic symptom had disappeared as soon as the mother understood its function and gave the needed emotional support.

It is rather unusual for one brief period of communication with a parent to suffice for giving the help that is needed. More often, the parent's attempts to follow the advice that has been given are impeded by his or her own unconscious feelings about the problem involved, and the parent needs more individualized help in gaining a perspective on the psychological factors at work in the interactions between him- or herself and the child. Any interaction between parent and child has meaning at several different levels. The surface level is always the most directly observable and the most obvious in its meaning. The deeper levels have meaning not only in terms of the dynamics of the child, but also in terms of the dynamics of the parent, and these can become obstacles to the child's development that are just as real as the physical limitations with which he must cope.

One particularly troublesome parental pattern that often goes along with the tendency toward overcontrol is that of possessiveness. It is easy for the mother who loves her handicapped child and who devotes large investments of time and energy to promoting his welfare to fall into the pattern of feeling indispensable to him and of even feeling an ownership of him. In order to give of herself to the extent required by his special needs, she must come to feel a deep gratification in being so needed. The need to feel needed is not in itself unhealthy. To the contrary, it is a constructive need which underlies much of the service given in this world. However, like all needs, it can become destructive in its effects if it is unconscious and excessive in degree. When this happens, a spider-like possessiveness spreads its tentacles to prevent any possibility of separation.

The phenomenon of separation between parent and child is one that occurs gradually, starting in infancy and extending into adult life. The newborn infant has no consciousness that he and his mother are two separate people. To him, her breast is a part of his own being from which he derives what his body demands. As he moves through the first year of life, the awareness begins to dawn that his mother is separate from him, and this is the beginning of his own emergent sense of personal identity. The development, reinforcement, and enhancement of that sense of personal identity constitute the core of his psychological growth and health as an individual.

During his first few years of life, the child is very closely identified with his parents. Their ways of functioning are unconsciously incorporated into the developing structure of his own personality. Their perceptions of the world in which they live become his perceptions. He sees things very much as they do. All of this happens in very intangible ways, without conscious direction or even awareness that it is happening. At the same time that his personality is forming through this process of incorporating the personalities of his parents, he is also developing patterns of reaction and ways of looking at things that derive from his own personal experience of life, both within the family relationships and also outside the home. As he gets older, his natural and psychologically healthy tendency to question the nature of things will lead to some areas of disagreement with his parents.

For most parents, the child's increasing separation into individuality is somewhat threatening. Most parents want their offspring to reflect their own viewpoints and attitudes toward life. To a large extent, this will happen naturally and inevitably if the relationship between parent and child is a loving one, but there will also inevitably be differences. These differences are essential and necessary if the child is to have a healthy psychological development. Not only will the growing youngster have opinions and attitudes that differ from those of the parents, but he will also *be* different from the image they want him to fit.

If the parents are able to be conscious of their own feelings and restrain their wish to overcontrol their child, the child will have less inner conflict about his own identity and less need to rebel against the parents in extreme ways. However, as a natural part of growing up, the youngster will need to assert himself against the parents from time to time and will need to test his separateness from them. If the parents are able to achieve a real acceptance of the child's growing individuality, they will permit him to express himself within the home and let him make his own choices as much as possible.

In the case of the physically handicapped child, the parents' unconscious wish to retain possession and control may be fed by the child's physical dependence on them. His physical dependence gives them a degree of power over him that they do not have in the case of their nonhandicapped children, and they may unconsciously relish this sense of power and possession. You may be shocked by this statement; but, if you think about it, you will realize that this is a natural human tendency which the parent can keep under control if he or she is able to face it consciously and work with it as his own inner problem. When this parental tendency remains unconscious, the physically handicapped child is particularly likely to become its victim.

Several of the parents in my therapy group made progress in the direction of accepting the importance for their handicapped child of achieving a sense of individuality and separateness. In Chapter Two you saw how a loosening of the bonds of emotional interdependence between Lois and her son Mark came about as a result of Lois' working through unresolved problems in her relationship with her own mother. Other parents in the group, observing the progress made by Lois and its beneficial effects on Mark, came to realize more fully that children may suffer from the failure of a mother to find her own identity and personal fulfillment.

One of the ways in which a handicapped child may begin to assert separateness from the parents is through forming attachments to other adults outside the home. When this began to happen, the parents in my group often felt threatened initially, but were able to achieve an appreciation of its value for the child. When Doris became attached to a neighbor lady, Jill thought at first that her own concern was about imposition on the neighbor, but then came to realize that she was feeling jealous. A similar reaction was felt by one of the fathers, Steve, whose son Ken became attached to a neighbor man.

Steve himself was a man who had found difficulty in achieving his own individuality and separateness, and he made real progress with this through the therapy of my group. A writer, he had for some years done his work at home, where he felt increasingly submerged in the family responsibilities and less able to function creatively. During one session, he announced to the group that he had gotten himself a little office downtown and that, by leaving home each morning and devoting his full day to his writing in his own separate place, he was better able to experience his own independent identity.

It seemed to me that Steve's physically handicapped son Ken really benefited from his father's progress toward becoming an individual. Steve had tended to be an overprotective father, and rechanneling his energies toward his own growth seemed to release Ken for the discovery of his own initiative. Steve told the group of how Ken had improved unexpectedly and markedly in some motor skill involved in a game the two of them had been playing together. While Steve had been looking in shops over a three-week period for some implement to make the game easier for Ken, the boy had been mastering the skill. Steve was greatly pleased by this spontaneous burst of motivation in Ken. A few years after my work with this group had ended, Steve came to my office for a private consultation about his son. Now in high school, the boy was asking for permission to leave Sunshine School, the segregated school he had always attended, in order to try to make his way in a public school. Steve's old lack of confidence in his son returned, and he felt sure the boy could not possibly make it in a public school.

"How can Ken ever know whether or not he can make it in the public school if he is not given the opportunity to try?" I asked him. Steve decided to set aside his own fears and let the boy try. Several months later he reported back to me that his son was managing very well in the public school. Steve had to admit that he was really surprised—but also glad—that he had not held the boy back.

The challenge that you face in enabling your handicapped child to actualize his own inner resources is a great one, indeed! Your love and caring for him must provide the basic satisfaction of his deep security-needs, so that he feels loved and cherished and valued and free from anxiety about abandonment. Within this security structure, you must give him freedom to develop his own capacity for self-direction. From an early age, the child is able to participate in choices of many kinds, such as which jacket he wishes to wear, which television program he wants to watch, which record he wants to play, and whether he would prefer a picnic or a trip to the zoo. Many parents include even their young children in family conferences when a decision is to be made that will affect the whole family. The fact that valuable contributions to family decision-making sometimes come from quite young children is

surprising to many parents. For the child who is limited in participating in so many of life's physical activities, other kinds of participation have a special importance. The knowledge that his
judgment is respected by you will enhance your child's sense of
self-esteem and increase the self-confidence that he will need for
finding his place in adult life.

CHAPTER NINE

Sunshine and Shadow

The meaning of life is something that each person must define for himself, and the way in which a person gives meaning to his life will profoundly affect the way in which he lives it. In talking with you further now about the special challenge which life has brought you, I shall be speaking from the framework of the meaning which life holds for me, and I hope that this viewpoint will be of help to you in your struggles. People do not arrive at their philosophy of life overnight or in one sitting, and you are probably in the process of finding yours.

For me, life has meaning as an opportunity for the experiencing and the developing of my Self. I capitalize the word Self because I do not use it in a self-centered way but rather in a way intended to connote the totality of my potential as a human being. This potential includes my ability to serve others and to contribute in constructive ways to the ongoing stream of life. But it also includes my capacity for experiencing pleasure and joy and the very personal gratifications of life. In thus giving meaning to my life, I am drawing not only upon my own thinking but upon the thinking of many philosophers through the ages and upon the thinking of certain writers in my own field of psychology. The concept of *individuation* (a process in which the personality develops through finding its own unique center, bringing more and more psychic life into the sphere of conscious awareness, and achieving harmony and balance between the unconscious and consciousness) as developed by Carl Jung and the concept of *self-actualization* (realizing inherent potentials and incorporating them into the self) as developed by Carl Rogers have affected me profoundly and have become deeply interwoven with my philosophy of life.

But I do not want you to think that my philosophy of life is derived primarily from the intellectual sphere. I am a human being who has lived with problems of many kinds and who has sought an understanding of the meaning of these problems. I have sought ways of living with myself in all aspects of my being, and I have found many paths toward development and personal fulfillment.

Like yours, my life also has been deeply involved with the problem of special handicap. Mine is a physical handicap, resulting from an extremely severe case of poliomyelitis when I was eight years old. For eight-and-a-half years, I was an extremely energetic and active child, bursting with eagerness for life against the bonds of parental overprotectiveness. Then, with appalling suddenness, the boom of darkness fell upon me and I was stripped of all movement except the turning of my head. The massive stone weight of complete paralysis enveloped my total body from the neck down. The only movement of which I was capable was the turning of my head.

Although I remember very clearly the onset of this total and terrible paralysis and the fatigue and irritability of the day or so preceding it, I do not remember the days that followed when I was enclosed in the delirium of critical illness and lay near death. Much later my mother told me that, when the crisis approached, the doctors stated that there was not the slightest hope for my survival. When I came through the crisis and lived, the doctors said it was faith and will power that had pulled me through.

I have no memory of that struggle for life, for it occurred within my unconscious while I lay in a state of high fever, but I have retained a conscious contact with the meaning of that struggle when the forces of life and death were pitted against each other in my very being. I have retained a childlike sense of the miraculous wonder of life, and I take nothing for granted. I value deeply my own capacity for appreciation of the gifts life brings to me and of the beauty of the world around me.

But I have also known times of dark engulfment in the black pit of depression when the blueness of the sky did not reach me and my strongest wish was for death. There were times as a child when I demanded bitterly of my mother, "Why didn't you let me die when I had the chance?" And there were times in my adult life when the gravity of seemingly insoluble problems annihilated my ability to make use of the muscular power that did remain to me in my impaired physical structure.

From the perspective of my present age and state of union with life, I look back upon *all* the experiences of my life with deep appreciation for their value in the process of my own development as a person. Who I am as a person—what sort of person I am—has always been of utmost importance to me. When I was a little girl approaching adolescence, I felt painful envy of the beauty, grace, and physical agility of my older sister, but even then I knew with complete certainty that I would never want to have been able to change places with her. I did not want to be anyone but myself, despite the terrible, unalterable impairment of my physical structure. From early childhood, I was involved in wanting to know myself and in wanting to continue to like the person that I knew myself to be.

No psychologically sound person would choose to have a physical handicap if this were in his power to control. Mobility and ease of physical functioning are one of life's greatest gifts. Having lost mine to the extent that I have, I know this fact much better than those who have always taken their physical mobility for granted. But almost every loss in life contains a potential for some kind of gain, and the question becomes that of whether one assumes responsibility for actualizing that potential.

My personal philosophy of life carries the conviction that the actualization of a person's potential must include his conscious experiencing of the dark side of life as well as its sunshine. Suffering comes to human beings in many, many different ways. For some people who are born in abject poverty and live out their lives in a desperate struggle for mere subsistence, suffering is of a constant, numbing kind which dulls the consciousness and allows little free-dom for personal development. For these deprived people of the world, the balance of shadow over sunshine is far too great, and help must come from more fortunate segments of the population if their inner potential for human and spiritual development is to be released from the imprisonment of their daily struggle to stay alive.

For many of us in the affluent society, however, there is suffi-cient sunshine in our lives that we tend to look at the advent of suffering as an unwelcome intrusion. If suffering comes, we ask, "Why should this happen to *me?*" as if *we* should be exempt from the rolls of sufferers. Yet, whenever I have met a person who has managed to live without establishing any conscious relationship to the experience of suffering, I have found that person to be vapid and superficial and limited by his inability to understand his own vague dissatisfaction with life. For life is full of paradoxes, and one of them is that the capacity for experiencing suffering and the ca-pacity for experiencing joy are two sides of the same coin.

When life brings suffering to us, we must choose between the alternatives of entering the experience head-on and trying to know its deepest and fullest meaning, or of turning aside from our own feelings and emotions with a denial that they exist and a pretense that we are unaffected by the dark side of life. It has been my experience that the degree of individuation which I have achieved has come as much out of the valleys of the shadow as it has from the sun shining on me near the peak of the mountain.

While I would not have chosen to be physically handicapped, I would not want to be without the inner development which I have achieved through this problem. I cannot give you the full story of my inner journey, for that would constitute a book in itself. But I would like to share some of my experiences which may be relevant to the problems with which you are living as the parent of a handicapped child.

I can still remember with great clarity the dawning of my realization that the crippled condition in which the polio had left me was permanent and that, while I would work to overcome it, I could never be completely freed from it. I did not understand this in terms of the nerves in the spinal cord that had been killed and could not be brought back to life or in terms of the bones that had been unalterably deformed, but I somehow knew that—while my feeble and tottering efforts would eventually pay off in regaining the ability to walk—I would never again run, and I had lost forever the joyous freedom of unfettered motion.

I was lying in my bed alone when this realization came to me. This was a bitter pill for a nine-year-old child to swallow and accept. While emotional *acceptance* of this unwanted reality was something which remained to be won and lost and won again in the tortuous uphill struggle of years ahead, there was a *confrontation* of the reality which I achieved at that time and which gave birth within me to a strength which I value as I value life itself. The same moment in which I most completely experienced my powerlessness gave birth to my inner strength.

Over the twenty years that I have been in full-time practice as a psychotherapist, helping adult patients with life adjustment problems of all kinds, I have found repeatedly that resistance against facing an unwanted reality has been a major block in the growth process of my patients. This applies both to the inner realities of a person's personality functioning and also to the external realities of his life circumstances. In Jungian psychology, we use the term "shadow" to refer to those aspects of a person's own being which he does not know and does not want to see. Only by getting acquainted with his own shadow and integrating it into his life can a person move toward psychological wholeness.

As long as the existence of an unwanted reality is not admitted, there is little that can be done toward achieving emotional acceptance of it and working with it in the most constructive way possible. The psychic energies which could be going into the achievement of acceptance and constructive adjustment are, instead, diverted into the processes of defending against awareness of that which one does not want to know. Involved in this kind of life problem is the question of how much power one has and exactly where one's power lies.

In working as a psychotherapist with people who are struggling to find their way through a maze of life dilemmas, I find that much of the work consists in helping these people to sort out the realities of themselves and of their lives in such a way that they can recognize what lies within their power and what does not. Some years ago, one of my patients who was also a member of Alcoholics Anonymous brought me a copy of the prayer adopted by that organization, and I have remained deeply impressed by the profundity of its message. It reads:

> God grant me
> the Serenity to accept the
> things I cannot change,
> the Courage to change the
> things I can, and
> the Wisdom to know the difference.

I have found that the serenity of acceptance necessitates experiencing one's own powerlessness, and that people fight against experiencing their powerlessness with an ingenuity and intensity that might better go into an implementing of the powers which they really do have. But the realistic and constructive implementation of one's powers to bring about change requires both effort and courage to risk the trying. Too often, human beings prefer to sit back in the comfortable aura of untested powers which they assume themselves to have while demanding that the effort be made by someone else. The wisdom to "know the difference" comes about through the testing of reality.

The physically handicapped person involved in testing out and developing the physical powers available to him has a wonderful opportunity for also developing a keen sense of reality. He is actively engaged in doing on a concrete level something which all people have to do with the less tangible aspects of life. The physically handicapped person who turns aside from the pain of facing his powerlessness and the responsibility of testing his powers will also turn aside from reality in its less tangible aspects and will live a withdrawn, unfulfilled existence. But the handicapped person who meets these challenges develops an inner equipment for the courageous discernment of *intangible* realities, too.

I owe a priceless debt of gratitude to my parents for the marvelous recovery I have made from a truly catastrophic paralysis. During the first few months of my illness, I had no realization of the permanence of my affliction, for I was too completely imprisoned by it to have any basis for perspective. Totally rigid and immobilized, I was turned on sheets by my mother for the purposes of bathing and nursing care. In the small rural town where I grew up, there was no hospital, and the medical services of the local doctor were supplemented by medical specialists from distant cities with whom he consulted about my condition. But the actual nursing care was provided by my mother, and my subsequent physical rehabilitation was carried on by my parents.

When the period of severe illness had passed and the tasks of recuperation lay ahead, the first hurdle was that of releasing my body from the stonelike stiffness which encased it. This was a difficult task for my parents to perform because it was so painful for me. Although my mother's nursing care had been so superb that there was no development of such possible complications as bed sores or constipation, I was emaciated and extremely sensitive to pain. This sensitivity to pain had been heightened during the early phase of the illness by the necessary use of large needles for medical injections into my wasted limbs. Yet, as I entered the period of convalescence, it was clear that no training of muscles or stimulation of circulation could be undertaken until the flexibility had been restored.

I have everlasting gratitude to my mother that she did not spare me this pain. My father protested, but she persisted. The warm, loving gentleness of my father toward me was one of the great gifts of my life, but I am glad that in this matter he did not prevail.

The stimulation and retraining of my muscular system was then begun and was continued throughout the years of physical maturation. For several months I was massaged two or three times every day, usually with my mother working on one side while my father worked on the other. While the frequency of the massage decreased with the passage of time, it was daily for many years.

The exercises were something which called for great effort from me, even in the early phase. I remember the months before I could sit up, when my mother would sit by my bed and exercise my hand. Supporting my arm in a horizontal position, she would raise my limp hand to a vertical position and I would try hard to hold it there. After several weeks, I gradually became able to hold the hand in an upright position for increasing periods of time, and eventually I became able to raise my own hand. In some areas of my bodily functioning, this work brought results and in others it did not.

In the period of the 'twenties and in the geographic area where we lived, there were no trained physiotherapists. Aware of the limitations of their own knowledge and concerned that I receive the best medical attention they could make available to me, my parents arranged for my admission to a church-sponsored children's hospital in a city in a neighboring state. On stretchers, I was taken on the train to that city and to that hospital. I remained in it for only a few days, and during that time my mother stayed in the city and visited me often.

I can only reconstruct from later accounts the story of my mother's decision not to leave me there. My own memories include being awakened during my first night there by the crying of another child. I listened silently as a nurse came in and chided the crying child, saying, "Hush up! You'll wake that new little girl!"

An older and somewhat more mobile girl lay on the bed next to mine; and, when my doll would fall over from its sitting position on the bedcovers, I would ask her to set it up again. A genial nurse engaged me in conversation and laughed kindly at something I had said, bantering, "You're full of prunes!"

"Yes, I am!" I flashed back in high humor. "I had them for breakfast this morning!"

My mother, meanwhile, was investigating just what kind of medical attention I was going to get and was disquieted by her findings. The medical focus seemed to be exclusively on the bone structure, with no provision being made for physiotherapy. It was apparently the intention of the doctor in charge of my case to use the weight of sand bags in an attempt to correct the deformity of my right leg. There was at this time some slight muscular rejuvenation beginning to show in my legs in response to our efforts, and my mother feared that this would be lost through the use of sand weights.

Desperately in conflict between her own best judgment and her respect for medical authority, my mother sought the opinion of another doctor and found support for her own viewpoint. This doctor commended her for the work she and my father had been doing to stimulate a rejuvenation of my muscles and advised her to take me back home and continue that work. This was done. It was many years later that the work of Sister Kenny in applying similar methods to the victims of polio became world renowned.

It was also some years later, when I was thirteen years old, that I spent one summer at the Shriners' Hospital for Crippled Children in that same city. This was a most beneficial experience for me in every way. It was only by happenstance that my father had learned of the availability of this treatment, and during the summer of my twelfth year we had visited the Hospital and talked with the orthopedist in charge. He was a loving and lovable human being who healed my soul with his warmth of feeling while he healed my body with his methods, which were an extension of those we had been using at home. It was his opinion that I had made a remarkably good recovery from such a severe paralysis and that I should continue working in the same way up to the age of full physical maturity in order to maximize any possibilities for recovery of muscular function.

That summer spent at Shriners' Hospital when I was thirteen years old did something very important for me in another way also. It enabled me to achieve a psychological separation from my parents, and this afforded me a basis for objective perspective which was invaluable during the individuation struggles ahead.

When my parents left me at the Hospital and returned to our home in an adjacent state, I was terrified. The residual effects of my polio are such that even to this day I am physically dependent on help in many essential matters, and at that time I was used to receiving all of that help from my parents, particularly from my mother. This physical dependence had resulted in an unusual degree of closeness with attendant emotional dependence in many ways. Although I had attended public school and had many friends among my peers in our little community, I had been excluded by my physical limitations from many of the experiences which normally facilitate the separation of child from parent. Now, when my parents departed and left me with strangers so far from home, I was very frightened and also experienced what we then called "homesickness."

However, as the days and weeks passed, I became involved in new relationships and new experiences and began to look at many aspects of life from a different viewpoint than before. As I stated earlier in this chapter, the experience of becoming crippled had brought me not only suffering, deprivation, and frustration, but also a potential for growth. One of the advantages which came out of my being physically limited was an enhancement of the ability to observe life and find meaning in it. When my parents came and took me home at the end of this summer away from them, I was surprised to find myself looking at our family life and seeing much to which I had previously been oblivious.

Young children live in a state of unconsciousness in which the human attributes of the parents are not scrutinized and criticized. Children act out their resentments and their rebellions against their parents, but they tend to do so without any conscious realization of what is happening in the relationship. Beneath the level of resentment or rebellion there usually lies a layer of guilt feeling based on a deeper unquestioned conviction that the parents are, after all, beyond reproach. The realization that parents are human beings, with their own adjustment problems and their mixture of constructive and destructive patterns of functioning, is a most significant part of growing up which comes at different ages for different people and sometimes never comes at all.

For me, the shedding of illusions of parental perfection was quickened by my summer away from home. It came at a most propitious time for me, as there were, at that time, developments in my family dynamics that could have submerged me in an unconscious emotional disturbance, from which I might have had even greater difficulty extricating myself, if I had not achieved the degree of objective perspective which I did.

All people have psychological difficulties of some kind, and those of my parents were manifested in their failure ever to achieve marital happiness or fulfillment. As individuals, each of my parents was a very sound person with integrity, courage, and many inner strengths, and my identification with them provides the structural foundation of my own personality. As parents, they were reliable and giving in a way that has been illustrated by their meeting of the challenge of my polio. Their deepest love seemed to go to their children, but that, like all blessings, had its dark side also.

My mother had grown up with and retained a deeply matriarchal orientation, which both contributed to and was reinforced by her marital disunity. One of the problems deriving from this was her inability to accept the psychological separation of her children as they passed through adolescence into adulthood and into their own separate lives. She could not have been completely unconscious of her own problem in this area for, during my younger years, she had talked with me many times about the difficulties she had encountered with *her* mother over her own attempts to individuate into adulthood and marriage. And yet, her conscious awareness was not sufficient to enable her to cope with her own inner conflicts when she was confronted with the attempts of her children to enter adult life.

These inner conflicts had erupted into her relationship with my older sister at the time of my return; and, as I observed the traumatic transition of my sister into the postadolescent period, I began to become aware of the connections between the patterns of my mother's functioning and the stories she had told me years before about her own mother. These observations and the inferences I drew from them proved to be of inestimable value to me at a still later period when I myself reached the threshold of adult life.

I was a peculiarly appropriate target for my mother's matriarchal possessiveness. This is very understandable to me now as I look back upon my childhood years and remember all that she did for me. Even then, I was keenly aware that my physical dependence burdened her, for she was overworked in the way that many housewives of that era were, keeping house with few conveniences and supplementing my father's income by sewing for the family and raising a small garden. Despite the fact that my younger sister was only a year old when I had polio, my mother carried the family responsibilities without help. Conscientious, and with high standards for her own level of performance, she never spared herself. Like most of the fathers of that day, my father saw his responsibility as solely that of breadwinner. While he provided the family transportation and was always very kind in what he did for me, he did not share the burden of domestic chores.

I therefore grew up keenly aware of the burden imposed by my handicap and overly reluctant to make demands. From early childhood, I had a strong and burning motivation to make my own way in the world. Even before the polio, I had identified with my school teachers and looked forward to the day when I would perform a similar function. Among the many severe losses which I suffered from the polio—which came in November—was the loss of the remainder of my third-grade school term. Throughout the following summer, I lived in great suspense over the question of whether I would be permitted to return to school in the fall. When the doctor gave permission and arrangements were worked out for the mechanics of my locomotion so that I could rejoin my class for the fourth grade, I was overjoyed.

During the years ahead, as I continued with my class through the public schools, there were many heartaches, many times of deprivation and frustration, many joys, and many triumphs. The fabric of one's life consists of many interwoven threads. I want to try here to delineate some of the threads of my relationship with my mother as they intertwined with my struggle for individuation into separate identity and more independent functioning.

There is a degree of dim ambiguity as I try to look back into the childhood years before the separation conflict had become overt. I was very fortunate to have parents who valued me in a way that nourished my sense of self-worth. The fact that I felt loved and that my courage and persistence were given verbal recognition by my mother strengthened my inner spirit and fed into an unspoken inner faith that I would eventually have a full life out there in the world.

At the same time I was aware that, at least partially, my mother did not really expect this to be so. Many times she would verbalize her worries about how I would get along once she was "dead and gone," and occasionally she would ask me with which of my siblings would I prefer to live after her death. Such questions were repugnant to me, and I would refuse to answer.

Intimations of the difficulties ahead also came at those times when my mother would complain about the fact that she had "sacrificed" herself for her children, and the implication was clear that her children were indeed obligated to her for that sacrifice. While the terms of the obligation were never explicated, and while I certainly could not have put them into words at that time, by my teenage years, I sensed that the implied obligation involved some kind of yielding of autonomy such that life would be lived under the domination of my mother's authority.

For me as a physically handicapped person, such a bond of obligation carried a particularly dire threat. With my outer mobility so limited, a surrender of inner autonomy could only have meant a loss of my vital connection to life. While my teenage years were very difficult for me in many ways, they were good years in the extent to which I was beginning to establish my own independent viewpoint and philosophy of life. This brought me into sharp disagreement with my mother on many issues; and, unfortunately, she was very threatened by my departure from her system of beliefs. This resulted in a decline of communication between us, so that the waning of the kind of closeness we had had earlier was not replaced by a new and more equalized level of communication. Instead, an emotional breach began to form.

My life at school was very important to me during these years. I had always loved the learning process, and it is fortunate that my parents never dispelled this pleasure by pushing me toward achievement. They took pride in my accomplishments, as when I graduated from high school as valedictorian, but I am grateful that they let my achievements be my own.

Although since my late teens I have been agnostic in my religious orientation, I have also always had a deep inner faith in the positive currents of the universe, which I now call God. I believe that, when I went through the life-death struggle at the age of eight and found my personal contact with the well-spring of life, I also plumbed an experiential basis for faith which has carried me through many times when the ambiguity of the road ahead might otherwise have overwhelmed me with anxiety.

Although it was never clear how college could be made possible for me either financially or in terms of the problems of locomotion, I never gave credence to the idea that college would *not* be a part of my life. One day during my senior year in high school,

I received a message to come to the office, and there I was introduced to the State Director of Vocational Rehabilitation. He told me about the program which he headed and offered me assistance in the form of payment of tuition and books at the state university. I asked if our neighboring states had such programs, and he replied that they did, based on certain residence requirements. Quite blithely, I then thanked him for his interest and politely refused his offer, explaining that I intended to go to the University of Utah instead.

Insofar as I remember, I had never before that moment explicitly formulated that intention. How I intended to do it, I have no idea, and I really had none then. The reason for my choice lay primarily in a novel I had read in which the University of Utah provided the setting. The town in which my state university was located seemed like a wintery and unattractive place, while I envisioned the University of Utah as the place of sloping green lawns and blossoming fruit trees which I indeed later found it to be.

I do not relate this with the specific intention of conveying a message or moral to the reader, for I am not sure what that message would be. Certainly I am a firm believer in the old adage that "God helps those who help themselves," and I have long been known by my friends as a very realistic person with a very sharp sense of the practical. Yet, in the last few years, I have come to recognize a quality of mysticism in my make-up also. As I look back over my life, I seem to see a kind of unfolding which was made possible by a reliance upon patterns of fate as yet undisclosed and calling for blind faith.

My blind faith that somehow I would go to the University of Utah seemed to receive confirmation when, not long after my graduation from high school, my father was notified by his company of an opening in a small community very near that university, and he applied for and obtained the transfer.

The reason that I now look back upon my choice of college as so significant in the unfolding story of my life is that I met my husband there. In a way, a fortuitous chain of circumstances brought him there at the same time I started. Six years older than I was, he had started college some years before and had gone for only one year before dropping out to join the Civilian Conservation Corps. These were the depression years, when many young men had to contribute to the family coffers, and it was only after several years of work that he was able to resume his education. Instead of returning to his previous college, he also came to the University of Utah, and we met in a class we were both taking the first quarter.

During the school term, we had frequent contact on campus; and, when he started taking me out in the spring, he had already decided he wanted to marry me. My husband is an unusual man of great depth and intuitive capacity and, more than anyone I have ever met, he was from the beginning able to see aspects of the inner me that were not readily discernible to others. It was as if he already knew me the first time we met. My handicap, rather than alienating him, had meaning for him in terms of his own relationship to early suffering of a different kind. Never one to be bound by conventional viewpoints, he already had a sense of values that pierced outer forms and went to the heart of the matter.

But I have now brought the reader ahead of my story. While fate had kindly placed me in close proximity to the university of my choice, she left to me the challenge of solving the other practical aspects of the problem. Immediately after moving to Utah, we contacted the State Department of Vocational Rehabilitation for educational assistance, and I was amazed to be told that I was foolish to think of going to college as my handicap was much too severe to permit either the rigors of college education or of professional competition afterwards.

The necessity for meeting the residence requirement of one year was clear and acceptable to me, and I was not unhappy with the prospect of spending a year at home while getting oriented to the new surroundings and trying out my skill at writing through a correspondence course. But it was my goal to become an English teacher, and I was totally unwilling to accept the assessment of my handicap as so severe as to preclude college attendance. I knew that I would be unable to get around the campus without help, but my old friend the Medical Director and orthopedist at Shriners' Hospital had told me of handicapped students on campus who had helpers employed for this purpose through the National

Youth Authority, a federal program for financial assistance to students.

The Department of Vocational Rehabilitation apparently used no psychological testing at this time for I was not tested, and evaluations were made entirely on the basis of interviews. The evaluation made of my capabilities was that I could not manage the challenge of college and that I should be trained for the job of mending hosiery in a department store! I still feel mildly angry indignation when I remember the director speaking to me of the money I could make from such a job, as if I were a child with a lollypop being dangled in front of my face!

The biographical annals of physically handicapped people are replete with instances of underevaluation of their capabilities, and I am sure that there are many thousands of unrecorded instances. It is essential for the physically handicapped person to have sufficient confidence in his own powers of self-direction that he will oppose such restrictive attitudes in constructive ways. This I did by setting about to convince the director of his misjudgment, by arranging for him to receive my school records and letters of recommendation from school personnel and other interested people. In the meantime, he agreed to support one correspondence course from the University. I learned that the University regulations did not permit this to be the desired writing course, as Freshman English was prerequisite to all other courses in the department. So I took my Freshman English by correspondence and the course in writing never did materialize because, when I entered the University a year later, I found myself compelled to change my vocational goal.

While I now look back on this change of direction as a stroke of fortune, it was a great blow to me at that time to be rejected by the School of Education. Again the basis of refusal was the severity of my handicap; and, in this instance, I see that decision as representative of wisdom on the part of those making it, for the kind of mobility needed by the public school teacher was beyond me.

Having finally agreed to subsidize my college education, the director of the State Department of Vocational Rehabilitation put the full weight of his support behind me and became a trusted friend. When I learned that it would be futile to take courses preparatory to teacher training, he arranged for me to receive vocational testing and counseling through the university, and this led to my decision to major in psychology. This was not a difficult decision for me to reach, for the dynamics of human personality and interactions had fascinated me since early childhood. The only deterrent to such a choice was the fact that, at that time, the field of psychology itself was still in such an early formative stage that future employment possibilities seemed dim. Again, I chose not to be dismayed by the ambiguity of the future and to take my chances in the field to which I felt attracted.

As I moved on through my four years of undergraduate study, I received advice from the chairman of the Psychology Department to plan to continue into graduate study with the goal of teaching on the college level, so my old love of teaching reentered the picture. By the time I actually did enter graduate study with my husband many years later, the war years had intervened and had given such an impetus to developments in psychology that the whole wide area of clinical practice had opened up.

Again, I am taking the reader ahead of my story. By the time I was on the road to professional specialization, the problem of being confronted by underevaluation of my capabilities was behind me, for my competitive prowess spoke for itself. But, returning again to the period of my entry into undergraduate college, we find that winning the assistance of vocational rehabilitation was not my last hurdle.

There were still others in positions of influence who saw my handicap as a preclusion to college attendance. It was not until the spring of my freshman year that I learned that the Dean of Women was not in sympathy with my attending. Her cooperation had been requested in the matter of assigning to me a student helper, for she had authority in the disbursement of the National Youth Authority funding through which the helper was to be employed. She agreed to make such an assignment and, in the meantime, I enlisted the aid of a friend who took me to campus for entrance examinations and registration. Friends in the suburban town where I lived also helped me to work out an arrangement for riding to and from campus with a carload of students. But the opening date of school came and went, and I still had no NYA helper!

Confronted with the necessity for containing my growing anxiety as each day passed, I telephoned the Dean of Women daily, and each day she told me she had not yet found anyone willing to take the job. At the end of two weeks, disturbed by the fact that I would be entering my six classes with the added handicap of late entrance, I called the Director of Vocational Rehabilitation. He said that he would look into the matter for me, and the next day I received a call from the Dean of Women, who gave me the name of my NYA helper and told me when and where to meet her.

I liked the girl who became my helper; and, although we developed different circles of friends, she and I were very compatible. In the spring, at the end of the second quarter, she came to me very much distressed and told me that she was resigning from this assignment. I asked her why, and she said that each time she reported to the Dean of Women she was put under pressure to talk me into dropping out of college and taking correspondence work at home. Rather than continue under this pressure, she had decided to change assignments.

Shocked and resentful, I considered the problem and decided to contain my feelings toward this Dean and concentrate on finding the solution. I discussed the problem with the students with whom I rode, and one of them offered to apply specifically for this job. This worked out and, as my friendships on campus widened, the problem disappeared. The Dean of Women apparently relinquished her efforts to influence my departure even though I didn't fit her image of the campus coed, and our various social contacts over the ensuing four years were smilingly pleasant though decidedly superficial.

My four years of undergraduate college became a time of great expansion for me in many dimensions. One very important area of expansion for me was the sexual sphere, for the college campus is a marvelous place for diversified contacts with members of the opposite sex. The most frustrating aspect of my life during my high school years had been my exclusion from participation in most of the heterosexual activities of my peers. While I had many friends among the boys in my classes, my physical limitations excluded me from many situations in which romantic developments typically occurred.

Although this fact may be surprising to many parents, high school youngsters are characteristically conformist. The high school peer-culture does not consider the physically handicapped girl among the most desirable romantically, regardless of her other attributes. The more cosmopolitan climate of a large college campus, however, loosens the restraints of conformity to a peer-culture and permits freer pursuit of individual interests in the heterosexual sphere as well as in the academic and other spheres. I found the college male to be less blocked by the existence of my handicap and more motivated to know the girl behind it.

As the heterosexual area of my development began to open, my mother was confronted with another challenge to her adjustment capacities in the relationship with me. As I have said, her own lack of emotional separation from her mother, her insufficiency of deep satisfaction in the marital relationship, and her persisting matriarchal orientation to life combined to produce in her a strong and predominantly unconscious resistance to releasing her daughters to adult life, and particularly to union with the opposite sex.

In her relationship with me, these problems were intensified because my continuing physical dependence on her reinforced her possessive view of me as *her child* and blocked her vision of me as a young woman separating from her and moving toward my own adult life. In fact, such separation was in reality impeded by my physical dependence and, during this period, I experienced the frustration of my handicap in new and particularly trying ways. Nevertheless, the expansion of relationships and activities outside the home did facilitate my psychological as well as physical separation from my mother, and my heterosexual relationships were primary in this development.

Much more than I then realized, my mother must have been caught in the trap of her deeply conflicting feelings about my heterosexual development. She had always loved me deeply and she honestly did not want to stand in the way of my living a full life, and yet her very being opposed my movement away from her. I clearly remember an incident many years later when my husband and I were solidifying our plans to move to California to undertake graduate study. At that time, the relationship between my mother and me had been very alienated for several years, and yet she said to me with a plaintive tone in her voice, "Would you *really* go to California and leave me?"

Before that point in time was reached, however, many tumultuous waters had passed under the bridge. Because my mother had early instilled in me her own great strength of spirit, I was in turn a high-spirited person and I would not yield to her domination. The crisis in our relationship came when my husband and I set our wedding date. Truly unable to let go of me graciously, aware that I would not yield to her control (and probably not really wanting me to), my mother resolved her terrible ambivalence in the only way she could, and that was by withdrawing from involvement with me. At a time when, in preparation for marriage and as a young bride, I was most deeply in need of maternal support and involvement at a new and different level, I met instead a coldly hostile rejection which clearly conveyed the message that if I went through with this marriage, I was doing so at the cost of sacrificing any hope for further love from my mother.

Always a vitally dynamic and inconsistent person, my mother reacted in this way despite the fact that her personal feelings toward the man whom I married had been positive from their first meeting. When Bill first came to our home in the spring of my freshman year, both of my parents immediately liked him, and he formed with each of them a deep bond of fondness which lasted until their respective deaths. During my sophomore year, when I was allowing myself time and experience before choosing a mate, the approval from my parents of my relationship with Bill was always apparent. Six years older and much more experienced, Bill had a depth of awareness of life that went far beyond that of most of the other young men I knew. The gift of his love for me was something that my parents could only respect.

When, at the end of my sophomore year, Bill and I solidified our engagement, my mother did not protest, for our marriage was a distant goal in the dim future beyond my college graduation. When, however, Bill graduated and we set our wedding date at the end of my junior year, the imminence of our marriage broke in upon my mother's consciousness with an impact which she could not absorb, and there arose between her and me a state of alienation that was never again dispelled.

Although she and I had occasional contact during the five years before Bill and I left Utah for graduate study at Stanford, we were never close and there was always an underlying coldness. From my present vantage-point of having done psychotherapy for almost a quarter of a century, I can look back and see how desperately in need of psychotherapy both my mother and I were at that time. There is tragedy in the fact that, although I eventually did move into the experience of exploring my own psyche and finding my own route to individuation, my mother had indeed sacrificed her own life. She never did discover for herself the route to personal fulfillment.

During the last decade of her life, my mother's physical health gradually failed. The close and dynamic interrelationship between the psychological and physical balance of the human organism has been repeatedly demonstrated for me in my clinical work, and I see my mother's early loss of physical health as a result of the lack of resolution of the inner conflicts which accumulated over the course of her life. She gave much, but no one gave her the help which might have provided the perspective from which to confront her inner conflicts and find her way through them. She died at the age of fifty-eight.

During our second year at Stanford, Bill and I went "home" to be with my mother at the time of a major operation. A year later, we went again—at the time of her death. I will never forget the terrible shock I experienced when I entered the room where she lay and saw how very emaciated she was. The ravages of her illness constituted a destructive power against which both she and I were utterly helpless.

And yet her marvelous spirit remained. At the moment of her actual death, the other members of the family had left the room and I sat alone with her. She had been in a coma, but she regained consciousness, raised her head from the pillow, and looked toward the door with a bright-eyed expression that could only be described as hopeful expectancy. Then her head sank back and her last breath expired. My mother had always been a religious woman with a belief in a "hereafter" in which she would be reunited with her early family. It was undeniably clear that she experienced the moment of death as a threshold.

It was during the ensuing year that the full impact of my alienation from my mother hit me, and I went into psychotherapy for the first time. This was a stressful time of inner personality re-organization for both my husband and me as we found it necessary to work, through psychotherapy, on the interaction in our marital relationship of the neurotic patterns contained in both of our personalities. I have since come to believe that this kind of therapeutic confrontation of the neurotic aspects of the marital relationship is essential to the achievement of marital fulfillment for most people, but that is another story. It is not an irrelevant story to our present subject for, in the fabric of a personality, all aspects of the life experience constitute interwoven threads. But the story is too long and complex to be included here.

Specifically relevant here to the matter of my relationship with my mother is the fact that, for some years after her death, I was ensnared in a web of guilt feelings which had to be brought to fuller consciousness in all its aspects before I could extricate myself from them. It is the way of life that, as one generation succeeds another, the offspring cannot repay the debt to the parents directly, but must instead move on toward the future, contributing to that future out of the font of experience provided by the past.

There is in man, however, a strong force which opposes such movement into the future and binds him to the past in a way that robs him of the very gift of creative productivity for which the past provided a foundation. In me, this atavistic force took form in a way which could be described as a voice saying: "You ungrateful child! You have no right to the pleasures and accomplishments of a good life that was made possible only by the sacrifices of your mother who now lies dead in her early grave!" The black clouds of guilt and depression were parted only by the light of acceptance of the fact that I am not responsible for the life pattern by which one generation succeeds another and each must in turn relinquish the future to the next.

The tragedy of my mother's life lay in the fact that she had had no help in dealing with her inner conflicts in such a way that she could move through them into an old age of fulfillment and contentment. There is no doubt in my mind that, as she found herself no longer needed by her children in the ways in which she felt able to serve, she relinquished the reins of her life and found it meaningless. The story has significance because it is a universal theme. The variations with which the theme is played out in the lives of different people are manifold. In my mother's case, her nonindividuated bond to her mother was transferred to a bondage in the relationship with her children, and she never freed herself to the extent that she could discharge her responsibility to herself. The problem of relationship to parents versus relationship to Self is a universal problem which, as a psychotherapist, I have found always to be involved in some way in my patients' difficulties in reaching a true fulfillment and understanding of themselves as individuals.

Insofar as any parent has unresolved problems in the relationship with his or her own parents, these unresolved problems will complicate and make more difficult the challenges and tasks of parenthood. Insofar as these problems are unconscious, the more dangerous they become in their potentially destructive effects. Sometimes it is the parent upon whom the destructive impact is greatest and sometimes it is the child. But it is the nature of the parent-child relationship that each affects the other. Fundamentally, however, it is the parent who must carry responsibility for the development of the child.

CHAPTER TEN

What Psychotherapy Can Do for You

Researchers have found evidence that parents of handicapped children avail themselves of psychotherapy less frequently than the general population. This is very regrettable, for not only these parents but also their children could derive great benefit from the broadened perspective of consciousness which psychotherapy can bring.

The fact that parents of handicapped children have tended not to view psychotherapy as an appropriate source of help stems from a fallacy in the minds of many people about the nature of psychological adjustment problems. Before the beginning of the twentieth century when Sigmund Freud was just introducing his psychoanalytic techniques, problems of psychological adjustment were identified with mental illness and were seen as occurring in only a small segment of the population. It is true that psychiatrists before Freud's time had distinguished between psychosis (mental illness) and neurosis, but their approach to the understanding of neurosis was simply to classify different kinds of symptoms, and it still was not recognized that all people enter adult life with some degree of neurosis. One of the great contributions of Freud was his focus on the dynamics of various neurotic patterns. Exploration into the meaning of these patterns led to the discovery that they arise from the unconscious efforts of people to deal with the emotional stresses and strains that are an inevitable part of living.

Such an understanding of the nature of neurosis invalidates the common assumption that, if a problem *really* exists *outside* of the person, he cannot be neurotic in his reaction to it. This fallacious assumption has been found to exist in the attitudes of many parents who point to the handicap of their child and, in effect, ask, "How can you say that I need psychological help when my problem obviously exists outside of me? The problem is the handicap of my child, and that is outside of my control, so what can psychotherapy do for me?"

The fact overlooked by these parents is that *all* neurotic patterns arise out of the impact of realities outside of the control of the person. The question most relevant to the psychological health of a person is that of how well he adjusts to that which is not within his control. The challenge is to find the inner means of adjustment that are most conducive to the constructive growth and development of the people involved. The purpose of psychotherapy is to facilitate this adjustment.

Such psychological theorists as Carl Gustav Jung and Carl Rogers have discovered in their therapeutic work with patients that each person's psyche contains the seed of his own optimal development. This psychic seed exists as a potential which may or may not become actualized to a significant degree. In every person's life, the forces which oppose this self-actualization are manifold, and life is never such that a person's seed of potential simply unfolds in an optimal and uncomplicated way. Indeed, it is difficult to know just what balance of gratification and frustration would best insure the optimal development of any person. The question is academic, for the realities of life are such that the development of a human personality *always* becomes an extremely complex matter.

From time to time, I have encountered the comment, "I would rather that life had brought me a physical handicap instead of these emotional problems" or "I would rather have a broken leg than an invisible inner disturbance." The implication of such comments is that life brings *either* physical *or* psychological problems—*either* concretely visible problems *or* inner disturbance. This is, of course, another fallacy. The fact, for example, that I grew up with a physical handicap certainly does not mean that I grew up free from any neurotic patterns of functioning. To the contrary, many of the neurotic patterns that I would have had anyway were intensified and complicated by the existence of my handicap. It is true, as I have stated earlier, that the challenges which my handicap brought me provided certain opportunities for the development of inner strengths which I might not have needed to actualize without such special problems. But it is also true that my handicap reinforced certain neurotic aspects of my functioning and added to the later difficulties of working them through.

The process of working through one's neurotic patterns so that one becomes free of them and able to move forward in the individuation process is, of course, part of what psychotherapy is all about. My own life is, in a sense, dedicated to a belief in the value of psychotherapy as a means of promoting psychological health in the world. The depth of my belief comes both from my own personal experience in working through my inner conflicts and finding my own route to individuation, and also from my professional experience of helping others to take their own therapeutic journey. For more than twenty years I have been involved in a full-time practice devoted primarily to individual psychotherapy with adult patients with all kinds of adjustment problems. The major way in which I have found my patients to differ from those people I know who have not had personal psychotherapy is that my patients tend to be more motivated to understand themselves and find healthier and more constructive ways of functioning.

When I was asked to undertake some group work with parents of handicapped children, I approached the project with the belief that the best way to help these parents would be through an application of the same methods that I used with other people. I realized, of course, that my work with these parents would be more limited in scope, both because of the group structure (as contrasted with individual psychotherapy) and also because the project would have a time limit, whereas people who come to me individually are free to continue working on their problems as long as they wish. However, there were also advantages in the group structure, because parents of handicapped children tend to feel set apart by a problem which the general population does not share.

These parents in my special group found it comforting to share their feelings with other parents with whom they had the common bond of a handicapped child. Nevertheless, as I had expected, the communication among these parents soon began to open up into other areas of their lives. Attention began to turn inward, toward clarification of their own emotional reactions and patterns of functioning. As they began to become involved in the process of their own development and growth as individuals, their ways of relating to their handicapped children began to change.

In Chapters One and Two, I presented the story of Lois' therapy, because it is a particularly clear-cut illustration of how the problem of coping with the child's handicap cleared up spontaneously through the mother's progress with her own underlying problem. There were other members of the group who had similar experiences.

One of these was a young wife, Peggy, who, together with her husband, Mack, entered the group out of a conscientious wish to discharge their parental responsibilities in the best way. Peggy's therapeutic exploration of her disturbed feelings about her little two-year-old, cerebral palsied daughter led to disclosure of her deep fears about possible social rejection of the child in the years ahead. This, in turn, led to an uncovering of Peggy's feelings that she had been rejected by her parents and treated as if she were inferior to her brothers. Unconsciously, she had begun to view her little daughter's handicap as proof of her inferiority, and she was trying desperately to gain acceptance of her daughter from her parents in order to offset these unhappy feelings.

Peggy made progress by removing her focus of concern from her daughter and working toward the resolution of her own unsuccessful struggle for approval from her parents. As she began to achieve a reorientation toward her life with her husband and her own children and away from her preoccupation with gaining acceptance from her parents, she was able to turn back to her relationship with her handicapped child on a new level. In the process of separating herself emotionally from her parents, she moved forward in her own individuation and became more aware of herself as a person in her own right. The marital relationship also improved, and she and Mack began to feel that they would be able to give their handicapped daughter whatever help she might need from them in the years ahead.

During one of the group sessions, Mack mentioned that he had found himself observing Nancy (the handicapped daughter) and had realized suddenly how much better able he was to understand the meaning of her behavior. He recalled then that, in a class for parents of handicapped children which he and Peggy had attended, they had been taught to observe the child, but he had never really been able to do this in a way that brought meaningful results. Now, as a result of their therapeutic work on their own adjustment problems, he and Peggy were finding themselves more sensitive to their child and the meaning of her behavior.

While the various members of the group differed in the degree to which they were able to utilize the therapeutic experience for their own growth, all of them found that their own particular way of experiencing the pain of their child's handicap was related to problems in their own inner life. Daniel, for example, was a man whose plaintively mournful vocal quality reflected not only his sadness about the cerebral palsy of his five-year-old daughter but also a generalized sense of disappointment with life. It was as if he experienced himself as one of life's less blessed creatures, and the handicap of his daughter seemed to him a confirmation of what he already knew. Many times during his months of membership in the group, he spoke of how helpful it was to know other people who had encountered misfortune in the same way; eventually the warmth of this support enabled him to look a little more deeply into the meaning of his feelings. He began to realize that he had always been plagued by insecurity in the area of his masculine identity; that is, he had always been unsure of himself as a man. The weakness of his father and the dominance of his mother had been factors contributing to his sense of inadequacy and failure. Without realizing it, he had been reacting to his daughter's handicap as proof of his lack of manliness. Daniel's period of membership in the group was not long enough for him to achieve full resolution of his inner problem, but he did gain sufficient perspective on it that he could be more objective toward the reality of his daughter's limitations.

Further illustrations are not necessary to convey the general point that the specific ways in which this parental challenge are most difficult vary and that they reflect problems in the individual parent's inner life. In talking with you as the parent of a handicapped child, I have tried to focus your awareness on the opportunity for growth as a person available to you by seeking the meaning within yourself of the difficulties you experience in this task of parenthood. In life, it is healthy to reach for joy and to build for fulfillment. But, when life brings you sorrow, that also has a value which can be utilized in your quest for wholeness.

Appendix

NATIONAL ORGANIZATIONS THAT HAVE LOCAL AFFILIATES SERVING HANDICAPPED CHILDREN AND THEIR FAMILIES

Epilepsy Foundation of America
Suite 1116
733 15th Street, N.W.
Washington, D.C. 20005
(202) 638-4350

Muscular Dystrophy Association of America
1790 Broadway
New York, New York 10019

National Association of Hearing and Speech Agencies
919 18th Street, N.W.
Washington, D.C. 20006

National Association for the Retarded
2704 Avenue E, East
Arlington, Texas 76011

National Cystic Fibrosis Research Foundation
202 East 44th Street
New York, New York 10017

National Easter Seal Society for Crippled Children and Adults
2023 West Ogden Avenue
Chicago, Illinois 60612

The National Foundation (*polio and birth defects*)
P.O. Box 2000
1275 Mamaroneck Avenue
White Plains, New York 10602
(914) 428-7100

United Cerebral Palsy Associations, Inc.
66 East 34th Street
New York, New York 10016

In addition to the organizations listed above, parents of handicapped children should contact the offices of federal, state, and local governments for information on the services they provide. Information on these many services may be obtained by telephoning nearby offices.